7/04

D1257845

GEORGES CHEVROT

SIMON PETER

SINAG-TALA
PUBLISHERS, INC.
Manila

©Original title in French:
Simon-Pierre

This Philippine edition was published in 1974 by Sinag-Tala Publishers, Inc. with special permission from Scepter Ltd.
Nihil obstat: Thomas O'Reilly, Vic. Gen. *Imprimi Potest:* ⁺Joannes Carolus, Archiep. Dublinen. Hiberniae Primas. Dublini, Die 17 Feb. 1959.

Second Philippine Printing, 1984

ISBN: 971-117-011-6

Cover: *The Denial of St. Peter*. Illustration by Gustavo Doré (1833-1883).

SINAG-TALA PUBLISHERS, INC.
P.O. Box 536
Greenhills Post Office
Metro Manila 3113

INTRODUCTION

WE have, here, collected together the principal passages of the Gospels that put our Lord and Simon Peter in each other's presence.

We do not hope in these pages to give a detailed account of the slow process by which Jesus fashioned the soul of the chief of His Apostles. The Master's patient moulding of His disciples is to be read in every page of the sacred narrative, and took place, above all, in those intimate conversations which He had with them " in the evening, in secret " (Matt, X, 27).

However, the collection of these few episodes throws a vivid light on the methods of spiritual education peculiar to the Saviour. We see Him using every means to discipline Peter's passionate temperament. Sometimes He reproves him roughly for his faults, sometimes He gives Him a chance to develop his good qualities, often He humiliates him or censures him, at other times, He praises him and encourages him.

If the art of the divine Master be used as a model by all who have charge of souls it will make us much more anxious to apply to ourselves the lessons that helped change the Galilean fisherman into the true disciple of Jesus, the model Apostle. By being a fellow-pupil of Jesus' with Simon Peter we will find the Master's teachings, not less difficult, but more realizable.

We recognise ourselves easily in the psychology of the ardent, impulsive disciple, who is now bold, now timid, but always loving, even in his weaknesses.

Peter is a sincere person. His integrity, his frankness,

his generosity win our instant sympathy. It is impossible not to love him, and perhaps his very imperfections help, rather than hinder, his being dear to us. We feel him to be so true, so spontaneous! As his failings resemble ours, so we are seized by a desire to imitate his virtues. Holiness, like his, is not forbidding; there is nothing mean or conventional about it. It is not a mask. Peter possessed our nature to the full, but he handed it over completely to the Saviour, and the love of Jesus Christ transformed him little by little in order to make him increase in virtue. In his presence, we no longer despair of reaching that state ourselves.

It is true that Peter's vocation surpasses ours. With him we can learn the rules of the Christian life and the apostolic tasks ; but in the Church He is our Head.

So the few lines of the Gospel, in which we catch a glimpse of the future Vicar of Christ, complete our Christian formation properly, by stimulating in our hearts, the Catholic virtues of trust, docility and affection for the Holy Church and its Head. How the problems of the day can be cleared up and reduced to nothing by considering in the text of the Gospel alone the key-bearer of the Kingdom of God !

The Gospel that allows us to admire the traits of Simon Peter's moral make-up only presents to us the shortest period of his activity. To see the Head of the Church in action one must, at least, look over the beginnings of his pastoral ministry in the Acts of the Apostles. To have a less summary idea of his sanctity, we ought to meditate on the doctrine of his Epistles. Then we would know *St. Peter*. We will attempt it one day, please God.

CONTENTS

Contents

Chapter V

Chapter VI

Chapter VII

Chapter VIII

Contents

CHAPTER IX

And I will give to thee the keys of the kingdom of heaven ; and whatever thou shalt bind on earth shall be bound in heaven ; and whatever thou shalt loose on earth shall be loosed in heaven.

        (Matt. XVI, 19)

CHAPTER X

At which He turned round and said to Peter : " Back, Satan, thou art a stone in my path ; for these thoughts of thine are man's, not God's "

        (Matt. XVI, 23)

CHAPTER XI

Peter said to Jesus : " Master, it is well that we should be here ; let us make three arbours in this place, one for Thee, and one for Moses and one for Elias ". But he spoke at random.

      (Mark IX, 4–5 ; Luke IX, 33)

Contents

Contents

Contents

Chapter XIX

JESUS CANNOT BE FOLLOWED AT A
    DISTANCE   167

*And those who had arrested Jesus led him away into
the presence of the high-priest, Caiphas, where the
scribes and elders had assembled. Yet Peter
followed him at a long distance, as far as the high-
priest's palace.*   (Matt. XXVI, 57–58)

Chapter XX

FROM IMPRUDENCE TO DENIAL   176

I do not know the man you speak of.
    (Mark XIV, 71)

Chapter XXI

REPENTANCE AND PARDON   186

*And the Lord turned, and looked at Peter ; and
Peter remembered what the Lord had said to him . . .
And Peter went out, and wept bitterly.*
    (Luke XXII, 61–62)

Chapter XXII

TO THINK WITH THE CHURCH   195

*The Lord has indeed risen and has appeared to
Simon.*   (Luke XXIV, 34)

Contents

CHAPTER XXIII

CHAPTER I

JESUS CALLS HIM

Jesus looked at him closely and said : Thou art Simon the son of Jona ; thou shalt be called Cephas (which means the same as Peter).

(John, I, 42)

THE fourth Gospel tells, in a few lines, the calling of Simon Peter. His brother Andrew and the author of this Gospel himself, till then both disciples of John the Baptist, learned from the Precursor who Jesus was. " Look, this is the Lamb of God ", he had said to them, pointing Him out.

They followed Him immediately and Jesus, turning around, asked them : " What are you looking for ? "

They replied : " Rabbi, where do you live ? "

" Come ", answered the Saviour, " and see ".

St. John will always remember this decisive moment in his life. It was about four in the afternoon, he writes. They spent the rest of the day with Him.

We are doomed never to know what was said in this conversation that began Jesus' ministry but, at least, we know that His two new friends left Him, convinced and rejoicing. *Invenimus Messiam.* " We have found the Messiah ".

What enthusiasm there is in this cry ! The Liberator, that Israel is waiting for, down through the ages : it has been given to them, to *them*, to live at the time when He has come into the world. Since their mothers taught them to pray they have been begging the Eternal one to send them Christ and now their prayer is granted.

1

The Messiah has appeared ! They have seen Him, they have heard Him ! It is to them, humble workmen, that He has spoken for the first time of the Kingdom of His Father. They have found Him Who is to snatch mankind from the servitude of sin and make the justice of God reign on earth. They were looking for the Truth ; they have found it. They were looking for God ; they have found Him !

How could they keep such a discovery to themselves ? They are too happy not to share their happiness. Each of them has a brother, a fisherman on the lake like themselves, and like themselves, a faithful follower of John the Baptist. They rush off to let them know.

Andrew, the Evangelist notes, was the first to meet his own brother, Simon. He announces his unheard-of luck to him : "We have found the Messiah" ! The Messiah ? Simon does not have to be told twice. Soon he is in the Saviour's presence.

Then, "*Jesus looked at him closely*". What an impression they must have made on the disciples, these looks of Jesus ! For, several times, the sacred narrative points them out as something never to be forgotten.

Jesus gazes at the newcomer ; He penetrates to the depths of his heart. Through and beyond the fisherman from Galilee, Jesus sees His whole Church to the end of time. He does not ask him to give an account of himself, He has known him always, He was waiting for him : "*Thou art Peter, son of Jona !*" As He knows his past, He knows what his future is to be. Simon has not yet recovered from the surprise of finding himself immediately identified when the Master adds "*Thou shalt be called Cephas*".

This introduction may appear strange enough to modern Westerners such as ourselves. It must have struck the witnesses of the scene vividly, more familiar as they were, than we, with the great memories of the history of the Chosen people. In olden times, God had, Himself, changed the name of the first head of the holy nation : " Thou shalt be called Abraham, that is, the father of a multitude ". Likewise, He had changed Jacob's name to Israel, that is " he whom God cannot resist ". With what mission would he be entrusted, he, the simple boatman who was being treated in such a solemn manner ? " Henceforth *thou shalt be called Cephas,* that is, a rock, Peter . . . . . . "

At present, *thou art Simon, the son of Jona,* you are a pious Israelite, faithful to the teachings of your fathers ; you live on the earnings from your fishing, as your people have done before you ; your horizons stop at the other side of Lake Genesareth. You hope to be the founder of a line of honest believers like yourself, and when you shall have raised them in the fear of God, they will take over your boat and close your eyes. However, God has other plans for you. You shall not die in the little town of Bethsaida, after blessing your children. You shall have a multitude of children. You shall cross rougher seas than that of Tiberias, for more difficult work than you ever dreamed of. God will change your life to such an extent that you will even lose your name ; *thou shalt be called Peter* for you shall be the rock, on which, for thousands of years, a thousand million men will be supported. *Vocaberis Cephas.*

The Gospel does not let us know the reactions of the future apostle ; besides, it is not these that are to instruct us, but the Saviour's word. A soul appears before Him and Jesus pierces it through and through. He sees its future, He names it, He consecrates it ; in a way, He takes possession of it.

Our Lord has His eye on each of us, also, for we all are, where God is concerned, the object of a special vocation.

* * * *

Thou shalt be called Cephas. To all men, Brethren, God gives names which correspond to His special intentions for each of them which fix them in their special places in His creation. God *names* us. He *selects* us. He *calls* us. He calls us to a task. He selects a function for us and that constitutes our *vocation.*

What is a vocation ? It is the particular task that God assigns to men. Other creatures receive a function that they necessarily exercise. Man, endowed with free will, also has his function to perform in the divine work, but he must fulfill it voluntarily.

On the other hand, in view of this special task that He gives to every man individually, God has endowed him with special abilities. But God does not give these qualities, required by our particular vocation, in their full flowering. He places their seed in our nature : it is our job to cultivate them and make them grow in the sun of His grace.

Although Simon will be well-named Peter, he does not change his character automatically with his name. He will not show overnight the firmness and constancy that his new name indicates. If his faith has the resistance of a rock, his will remains a shaking stone for some time longer ; one day, Jesus will even tell the man whom He wants to make the foundation stone of His Church that he is " only a stone in His path ".

In calling us to a task, God does not suppress our activity, He stimulates it. He calls us but we must respond.

By the fact of our baptism, we are all what St. Paul called his brethren : " *vocati sancti* " : we are " named " saints. Not actually " become " saints *ipso facto,* but called to holiness and capable of attaining it.

Likewise, there are particular functions that God

assigns to different people. Those who are " named " spouses and fathers may not refuse the obligations of their charge afterwards, under the pretext that they were not cut out for the exigencies of conjugal life or that the stuff of an educator was not in them. In calling us to a certain state, God gave us the capacities which that situation requires but it is up to us to develop them. Simon became Peter only at the cost of renewed and progressive efforts : neither shall we acquire the virtues of our vocation except by dint of energy and patience.

God will never do for us what we can do on our own. Certainly, He could transform us without any co-operation on our part because He is the Creator. But in that case there would only be creation. " Vocation " adds the free response of a human creature to the creative action.

The Lord asks us : " *Do you wish to enter into life*, to enter into the plan conceived by the Author of Life ? Do you wish to do your part in the divine work of life ? Do you wish to understand and direct your life, to lead a full life and to receive in exchange the fulness of life ? Do you wish to follow Me ? Do you wish to be perfect ? . . . . *Si vis ad vitam ingredi. Si quis vult venire post me . . . . Si vis perfectus esse . . . .* "

Here God does not impose, He proposes. When He created the irresponsible universe, it was enough for Him to say : " Let there be light ", for millions of lights to illuminate space. But having made man a moral being He must respect human personality. He asks, He calls : " Do you wish to become the light of the world ? Do you wish to lighten your brethren and glorify your Creator ? "

No more than the Lord transforms us in spite of our-selves, can we transform ourselves without Him. A vocation implies a collaboration of God and man. God helps us to transform ourselves ; He helps us powerfully and unceasingly. The mysterious but real help of grace comes to the aid of our natural resources both to accentuate the native dispositions that we bring to the accomplishment of our task and to correct the tendencies that would make us deviate from our vocation.

The divine assistance does not occur in the interior of our souls only. God, the master of events, makes them serve what He expects of us, even when they are the result of our defaulting and rebellious liberty. Is not this how the Saviour acted as regards Simon Peter ? He used His apostle's errors of judgement, his imprudence, even his denial, to prepare him more fully for his mission. In the same way, our rebuffs, our imperfections and our faults are so many lessons that make it easier for us to observe our pending duties, and which will help us to become what God wishes us to be. Fr. Faber wrote this thought-provoking sentence : " Our past years are a volume of prophecies ". For many, alas, these prophecies come true with a rigid exactitude, because they just renew their past faults monotonously. But, for whoever knows how to profit from his mistakes, past faults (really, healthy predictions) are warnings that put him on his guard and keep him from falling again.

The help that God gives us to carry out the tasks, He allots to us, we find, in the end, in the task itself (for it arouses the virtues that are necessary to it and hastens their development). When our task comes from God and not from our ambition, it carries with it the qualities that we need in order to perform it. Are there any parents who have never felt, in themselves, the miracle of the first cradle ? Before the little being, who needs your devotion, your mutual love is suddenly increased. Till then, your affection had no other end but itself but the child quickly rids it of that unconscious excess of egoism that would have proved fatal to your very tenderness.

Likewise when you occupied a subordinate position you were not afraid to take certain foolhardy risks which you would not dare to take later on when you reached a position of responsibility. It is only then that you discovered in yourself the virtue of prudence which perhaps you had never tried to develop before.

Life, as God forms it for us, is an educator to which we would do well to listen, for it tempers our character. Illness, that inexplicable illness, comes just at the right moment to teach us to be more sympathetic to the sufferings of others. Our dreams (so incomprehensible, too, when one has so much trouble already in performing one's task well), God uses to detach us from what is perhaps a false understanding of our true interests.

God goes as far as breaking us off from our own opinions. As we advance in age, we correct those beliefs and ideas that seemed to be a very part of ourselves. Some " put water in their wine ", others, on the contrary, like their drink with spirits added to give it body. Those who are cheeky grow wiser, the timid become bold. The philantropist learns how to pray one day, while the man who is exclusively faithful to his religious duties is given over, more and more, to works of charity. And all explain their evolution in the same way : " Life has changed us ".

In reality our opinions were, unbeknown to us, imposed on us from without. Life strips us bit by bit of these unfamiliar chattels and makes more exact notions of truth rise up in us. God has ordained everything so that our life may furnish us with the means of conducting it well.

One might object that this transformation is far from being universal. That proves that it is not inevitable. It only takes place in those who want *to live their vocation*. But, from the moment that a man consecrates

himself to his work, his work modifies him and, if that
work is good, it will make him better. And when,
not as a man any more but as a Christian, he delivers
himself over to his Christian vocation, it does not delay
in making him holy. Simon effaces himself before Peter
as John the Baptist found his happiness in decreasing
as Jesus grew in stature, as St. Paul rejoiced to be no
longer the master of his life since Jesus had come to
live in him.

*   *   *   *

It is important, therefore, that we should have a
very keen consciousness of our vocation. The indispensable effort needed to *accomplish* it is made easier by
the effort that we make to *recognise* it. Simon is no
longer the same once Jesus has given him the name of
Cephas.

What is our vocation? It would be good, dearly
beloved, if you would re-read, for example, on the
anniversary of your Baptism or your first Communion,
the prayers of the baptismal liturgy. Their boldness is
appropriately overwhelming ; at the least, they show up,
without any possible shadow, our Christian vocation.
They come back to that unparalleled declaration that
Christ addresses to the neophyte, who, from then on,
is one with Him : " You were the son of a man, from
now on you shall be called *the son of God* ".

For the name that God gives us is our true name. It
is neither a metaphor nor a simple title of praise ; beings
are in fact what God decides to call them. We are sons
of God. Sons by adoption, but really sons, made
children of God through the blood-brotherhood that
Baptism makes us contract with Jesus Christ Who is,
by His nature, Son of God.

That is what it means to be baptised. A baptised

person is not the lovely baby wrapped in white, of whom one cannot tell whether he looks like his father or mother. This little child has just been marked with a different resemblance ; he resembles his elder brother, Jesus Christ, and his life ought to be an everyday attempt to reproduce this resemblance voluntarily.

To be baptised is not to be entered on the Church registers and to find oneself officially a member of a religion. A baptised person is a child of God for the rest of his life ; a well-behaved, loving, generous child, or a negligent, disobedient, unnatural child, but as long as he is on earth, God will name him as His child and Jesus Christ will call him His brother.

No, a Christian is not a man like other men. So he ought not live like the others. We will only be co-heirs of Christ in the beatitude of Heaven on condition that we act like children, that is to say, be *collaborators with God* now, continuing the work of our elder Brother, both in our personal life and in the influence that we exert around us. That is our vocation.

This general vocation is *specialised* for each of us. God, Who never repeated Himself in creating the leaves of a tree, attributes to every man his individual form of life. We have a unique role and place in creation. We are not anonymous or interchangeable. God knows us by our name and each of us receives from Him a determined and fixed task which is different from that of our neighbour. I must do the work that He has allotted to me in the position in which He placed me. God needs me for the realisation of His plan ; in some way, I am necessary to Him.

Vocaberis Cephas—Simon must not take James' place, even out of humility, even for the sake of a prompter martyrdom. Simon ought to stay in the special place that Jesus assigned to him : Cephas is necessary to Jesus. We all, therefore, belong to God and we are His children in a unique way and God belongs to us and He is our Father by a unique title.

The conditions of our birth, our station in life, our profession, create duties for us to the extent of marking out our *particular vocation* and expressing God's special will for each of us. There, in the special place that God has put us, we ought to collaborate with His work with all the love of a child.

Even more so, every prayer that we address to God ought, as its first aim, to teach us *our vocation of the moment*. Day after day, hour by hour, God lets us know our task as children of God and as brothers of all mankind.

God never stops " calling " us. We do not always hear His voice because of the tumult of the varied occupations that waste our time, or because of the noise of our passions. But as soon as we recollect ourselves, we hear that voice of God that lets us know His present will. He calls us to prayer or to charity, to action or to sacrifice, by unobtrusive inspiration or by the pressing solicitations of the invisible and loving host of our hearts, the *dulcis hospes animae*.

One asks oneself whether one is not dreaming in hearing such a programme set forth ! But we only enumerate the rudiments of Christian dogma. Whoever does not understand that is ignorant of the whole of Christianity.

Does not our Baptism confer dignity on us ? Oh ! may we not be the sort of Christians at whom Henry Heine jeered, remarking that the water of their Baptism had dried very quickly. Let us set ourselves bravely to deserving the name that Jesus Christ has given us ; to bear proudly, without degrading it, our admirable name of " Christian ".

CHAPTER II

THE NEED FOR A FRESH START

*Master, we have toiled all night and caught nothing
but at Thy word I will let down the net . . .*
(Luke, V. 5)

IT would be right to think that after the definite call
that Jesus addressed to him, Simon Peter was one of
the disciples who accompanied Him on His first evangel-
ising journeys. But in between times the disciples
returned to their usual occupations. This explains how
we find them again, some months later, on the shores
of Lake Genesareth, in the middle of washing their
nets, in a bad mood no doubt, because they have had
no luck : they did not get any fish the night before.
It was useless lowering and raising their nets ; every
time they brought them up again it was to bring up
weed, mud, insignificant small fry, otherwise, nothing to
speak of. *Nihil cepimus.*

This is the moment that Jesus chose to attach them
definitively to His ministry and His person. The crowd
was already with Him. " He went through all Galilee,
teaching in the synagogues and healing the sick whom
they brought to Him ". The people did not tire of
hearing Him.

That day, Jesus had brought His listeners close to
the lake and while they crowded around on the bank,
He went on board Simon's boat and asked him to row a
few strokes out so that, being a little further off, He
could be heard better by all. When the Master's discussion was ended, Peter wanted to take Him back to
the shore but Jesus stopped him. " *Stand out into the
deep water* ", He said, " *and let down your nets for a catch* ".

11

Men of any craft can never stand laymen giving them advice on matters relating to their profession. Simon must have looked Jesus squarely in the face (of course, Jesus was different, but what an idea, all the same !). First of all, there weren't any fish ; secondly, what a time to go fishing, in the middle of the day ! And they had just spent a wasted night and tiredness made them feel even more that they had given themselves bother to no purpose ! Simon was used to speaking as he thought, " *Master, we have toiled all the night and caught nothing* . . . ." But already he regretted his first impulse. Could anyone resist Christ's word ? He protests but recovers his temper immediately : " *but at Thy word I will let down the net* ". He makes a sign to his companions ; the fishermen stretch their muscles again and pull away from the shore.

While they row, the disciples are thinking to themselves . . . " If, after all, we are going to bring fish back (for hope in the human heart is stronger than doubt) . . . After all Jesus changed water into wine at Cana. Since God speaks through His mouth . . . . . . But what will the others say if we come back with fish ? . . . . . ."

Jesus is thinking His own thoughts as well. He will soon have to lay the foundations of His Church and here are the men who must preach the Kingdom of God to a world given over to materialism, a world that only believes in money and strength. These are the poor fellows who will have to hold their own against the Synagogue and Imperial Rome. These are the men whom He will send to rescue humanity with the sole weapons of love and sacrifice ! It is mad what He is going to ask of them ! He is going to impose a super-human task on them, He is thrusting them into an impossible adventure . . . . .

This is, indeed, why the Master has to convince

them that with Him they can even undertake the impossible. Simon already understood it : " *in verbo tuo* ". The moment that Jesus orders, he sets out. He will have to set out also, with the same confidence in the Divine word, when he hears the final command : " Go, make all nations my disciples . . . . . I am with you till the end of the world ".

The lake is now deep enough. Simon throws out his net, and it falls on one of those shoals of fish that geographers tell us occur frequently in Lake Tiberias and which sometimes cover almost an acre of the surface.

The cork floats disappear in the water, the net is filled to breaking point. Now, here is another headache : how will they get it back in ? Their comrades in the other boat are hailed, they rush over. Carefully, the heavy burden is hauled in and divided between the two boats, which struggle back to the bank, looking every minute as if they will founder under the impossible load of fish . . . . .

Before we hear Simon Peter and the Saviour drawing their conclusions from this miracle, let us apply, Brethren, the first lesson that the Master and His disciple give us. All the members of the Church are " called " ; we have recognised the beauty and the urgency of our vocation as Christians. But we are not merely called once for everything ; all the time, Jesus is " recalling " us to the duty that He expects of us. The development of our spiritual life, like the efficacy of our apostolate, demands, on our part, perpetual " fresh starts ".

Duc in altum ! Stand out into the deep water, Jesus says. Face up to contradictions. Go back where you came from. Begin again . . . . . The secret of all progress and of every victory is, in fact, to *know how to begin again,* to learn from a failure and to try once more. To begin again, not by reproducing old relapses, but to begin again by getting rid of the first mistakes, by correcting former imperfections ; to do better, to advance more deeply, to raise oneself higher, " *Duc in altum !* "

Genius is patience, which does not leap to conclusions after vain attempts, but only after efforts made again and again, and which improves itself unceasingly. The scientist goes back over his calculations and renews his experiences by modifying them until he has found the object of his research. The writer shapes and reshapes his sentences twenty times. The sculptor breaks one rough model after another, as long as he cannot express his interior vision. In order to obtain the enamel he wanted, Bernard Palissy rebaked indefinitely. The poor fellow did not have enough wood to keep his kiln warm, and he threw his furniture into the fire, even the floor-boards . . . . . . All human creations are the result of unwearied new beginnings.

One must expect to meet this law again when it comes to spiritual creations. If the musician only becomes master of his instrument after years of patiently renewed exercises, can we hope to acquire mastery of ourselves otherwise than by repetition of virtuous efforts, of ever-growing difficulty ?

The author of the *Imitation* points out for us the true motive of moral mediocrity in those who give up too often, " *horror difficultatis, seu labor certaminis* ", dread of difficulty or the hardships of the struggle[1]. We correct a fault only on condition that we fight without a pause, and the battle tires us. We only progress in virtue by surmounting new difficulties all the time, and our nature loves what is easy. In the meantime, we would like to perfect ourselves . . . .

We would like . . . . . ! Oh ! that fatal conditional tense of wishers ! The people who succeed are those who have only conjugated the verb " to want " in the present tense : I want. I want the means because I

---

[1] *Imit.* Bk. I, ch. 25, 3.

want the end. I always want, even if the results are a long time coming about. I still want, even though the results are insignificant, or nothing, or, perhaps, contrary. " Courage is more necessary than time to make a saint ", noted Fr. Olivant in his book of Retreats.[2]

Now courage consists of beginning again with a new effort, beginning again even after retreating. Our most certain advances often follow rebuffs if, instead of meanly taking the part of our faults, we know how to draw profit from them for a new beginning, more humble and more expert. Perseverance, we must always insist, does not consist in never falling but in always raising oneself up again.

Let us apply Marshal Foch's maxim to our spiritual battles. When he was hurrying up the last offensives, he replied to the Allied leaders who asked for a little respite for their worn-out troops : " Victories have always been carried off by tired soldiers . . . " Let us tire ourselves in beginning again.

Duc in altum . . . . . . Simon, go back where you came from. To begin again, in the spiritual life, is to resume the interrupted work and not to get caught up in some other. It is not, unless exceptionally, to change direction, or director, or state of life, but to recommence life with a more courageous and newly youthful soul.

It can happen that we need, at times, to correct our methods of spirituality or of action, but let us not lose sight of the fact that our past defeats belong, above all, to ourselves, who did not know how to, or did not want to, use the means that Providence offered us. After that, we should be badly advised to call them defective.

To begin again is to do the same thing again by applying oneself to doing it better. Therefore, let us (a) apply ourselves better to exercises of piety before we increase their number or prolong their duration,

† R.P., Olivaint. *Journal de ses Retraites annuelles.* vol. I, p. 10.

(*b*) engage ourselves as closely as possible in an efficacious struggle against our dominant fault, before we tackle some other, (*c*) realise more often our intention of serving God, (*d*) put new life into the fervour of our good desires.

Duc in altum! Simon, go out even further than you went during the night of vain effort . . . . .

That is to say, Christians, let us enter more deeply into the Christian life, let us attempt to raise ourselves higher. To advance in virtue we must not be afraid to see and to wish " big " ! By aiming simply at ordinary decency, we will never pass mediocrity. Let us soar to the heights. Fr. Surin wrote : " If I am pressed to say why there are so few saints, when there are so many people who try to serve God, I will reply that the true cause is this : " Our aspirations are not high enough ".[1]

Let us always aim higher. To be sure of not committing any more mortal sins, let us cut out deliberate venial sin, for whoever consents to the latter will come, inevitably, to fall into the former. You have resolved not to backbite your neighbour any more : get used to speaking well of him. Let us always have in mind more than our strict duty. Come to that higher degree, we will find there other heights more elevated still. God would not show them to us unless He had called us there and we were capable of attaining to them. A Christian, disciple and member of Christ, is a man who is made to surpass himself.

But do not suppose, as the *Imitation* warns us, " that you can always maintain yourself in the same degree of virtue, when an angel in Heaven, and the first man in paradise lacked that perseverance ".[2] After having been able to accomplish a splendid sacrifice, one is sometimes bowled over by a tiny temptation. What then ? . . . then there is nothing for it but to begin again.

---

[1] R.P. Surin, *Traité de l'Amour de Dieu*, Bk. I, Chap. 10.
[2] *Imit.*, Bk. III, ch. LVII, 3.

" We will discover, I believe ", said Fr. Faber, " on the Last Day, that many heroic and saintly lives were simply a long chain of generous beginnings ".[1]

As much as our personal sanctification, apostolic action ought to find us ready to begin our endeavours again in a patient spirit. The good educator is the one who repeats the same thing a hundred times ; but never at the wrong time (nothing is more discouraging for a child than a discouraged or irritated teacher). " It is, above all, when one prays for others, that patience is indispensable ", observes Mgr. Gay.[2] Prayers, examples, persuasions, generally, only lead to the conversion of a soul if we renew them indefinitely without letting ourselves be put out by their apparent inefficacy.

Let us take the activity of the Church as a model. She is always in the process of beginning again. Her goods are confiscated, Her buildings are closed, She rebuilds others. She is always busy building temples, schools, charitable homes. If her institutions, her works, which share in the evolution of societies, have become obsolete, unworkable She does not stick there ; She creates new ones, better adapted to the difficulties of the day. The Church, which is promised eternity and whose dogma never varies, never believes, in the work of Her apostolate, that She has created an absolutely binding precedent. She is always perfecting Her means of conquest with her own art of blending, in their exact proportions, the traditions to be maintained and the progress, which will improve those traditions. Like Her first Head, She is always starting again to throw out the nets, because like Him, She believes the word of Jesus, " In verbo tuo ".

*　　*　　*　　*

For Simon Peter has just taught us the means of

[1] Faber, *Oeuvres posthumes*, vol. II, p. 235.
[2] *Vie et vertus chrétiennes*, chs. XVI.

resisting discouragement no matter how great our lassitude. Jesus says to us : " *Courage !* " St. Peter tells us : " *Confidence !* "

Actually, common sense and experience should be enough to convince us that one needs to begin again. The virtue of hope drives us to it invincibly. But there is the terrible contradiction of the facts, the " bad luck " that dogs our footsteps, the very faults that are repeated, the failures that regularly bring our enterprises crashing down. There are also the days when one has a good mind to chuck the whole game. What good is it beginning again only to founder every time ? Let us repeat then, Brethren, the three little words of the Apostle : " *In verbo tuo* ".

Yes, humanly, everything is finished. I can do no more, and I do not want to do any more. But it is You, Lord, Who order me to set out again. I will set out again, therefore, not because it seems reasonable to me, but because You order me to do so. Immediately our action is elevated on to a supernatural plane, where human considerations are of no further value. We begin again *not in order to succeed, but to obey. In verbo tuo !* I don't want to act any more but, my God, make of me, make in me, make through me, what seems good to You. It is not my work that I am accomplishing, it is Yours. This change of perspective gives us dispositions of humility and disinterestedness and courage which favour the divine action in us and which allow the miracle to take place.

To correct myself, to perfect myself ! I have exhausted myself in vain for so many years ! I will begin again this time because it is necessary, because God wants me to eliminate sin from my life, because Jesus wants His Christians to be like Him. (Our Lord wants our sanctification much more than we do). The indispensable but sure condition of progress is that God be there at the beginning, at the middle, and at the end. Many people do not progress because they have taken the wrong route, the one that ends in " ME ". They would like to be good, because it pains them to fall short of their ideal. This is only a round-about form of the cult of oneself.

If, on the contrary, we wish to obey God only (to imitate Our Lord, not to gain more moral beauty but because He loves us ; to fight against our natural imperfections, not because these destroy the balance of our character, but because they make the Holy Ghost, Who is in us, sad), then we are on the true road to holiness.

God raises us there higher than our hopes. St. Paul says it : " He whose power is at work in us is powerful enough, and more than powerful enough, to carry out his purpose beyond all our hopes and dreams ".[1]

Similarly, He will perform marvels through our apostolate, *if we are not preoccupied with succeeding, but only with obeying*.

The educator who has the misfortune to be ambitious for personal success, or even only for recognition ; the apostle who wants to prove himself right against the unbeliever with whom he is discussing ; the person who gives good example, hoping that he will be followed ; all these have already been paid their wages. When one looks, one finds, that is to say that at the *end* of one's efforts, one finds nothing. *Nihil cepimus*.

But when the apostle is not ambitious for personal success, when he is only absorbed in the sorrowful thought that souls are being lost, souls redeemed by Jesus Christ like his own, it is no longer the man who acts, but Christ Himself, and the unlikely is no longer the impossible.

The Church furnishes us with another proof. Was

---

[1] Eph., III, 20.

She given over to despair when a persecuting Legislation in France reduced Her and impoverished Her ? To-day, in spite of the lamentable decrease in the birth-rate, many dioceses see the number of priestly vocations increasing. It was attempted to take the children from Her, by withdrawing the right to teach from members of Congregations, and now official teaching gives to the Church, year after year, a more and more numerous élite of young apostles. More cunning still, anti-religious tactics succeeded in detaching the mass of the workers from the Church, and we see to-day in the ranks of the young workers, more than apostles, authentic saints blossoming forth.

See, by what miracles Our Lord responds to the confidence of His disciples. Let us, therefore, always have confidence, even in the face of what seems to us to be impossible. Confidence when it is a question of perfecting ourselves, confidence when it is a matter of making our Gospel known and loved. Don't let us delay in weighing our chances. Don't let us be dismayed by the difficulty of the gigantic tasks that are imposed on our insufficiency. Like St. Paul let us rejoice in our powerlessness. It is when we feel our weakness that the power of Christ comes to dwell in us.[1] Like St. Peter, let us go boldly to every task that Jesus sets us, by His word, " *In verbo tuo* ".

---

[1] II Cor., chs. XI and XII.

CHAPTER III

THE APOSTLE'S TASK

Henceforth, thou shalt be a fisher of men.
(Luke, V., 10)

THE miracle of the fishes produced a stunning effect on the future apostles. Simon Peter fell down and caught Jesus by the knees : " Leave me to myself, Lord ", he said, " I am a sinner ".

These two lines of the Gospel paint the whole man. The idea of being flattered at divine favour does not occur to him for an instant, on the contrary, he does not understand how he could be its object, he, a sinner. He has never seen his unworthiness so clearly as at this moment when God shows him particular benevolence. Bourdaloue remarks it in connection with St. John : " Nothing made the saints more humble than the favours and graces with which God honoured them . . . . . . The sight of their sins alarmed them, but the sight of the graces which they were continually receiving, and which they were afraid to abuse, astonished them no less ".[1]

Meanwhile, Simon Peter has another feeling, no less lively, for instead of backing away as his words might lead one to expect, he throws himself at the Saviour's knees. (St. Luke does not say that he kneels before Jesus, but that he throws his arms around His knees). He tells Jesus to go away from him, and at the same time he stops Him by holding His legs. " *Leave me to myself, Lord !* " and he hugs Him tighter.

This mixture of humility and affection, my Brethren, is a characteristic of fervent souls. The Church seeks

---

[1] Bourdaloue, *Sermon pour la fête de Saint Jean l'Evangéliste.*

to inspire us with it, when we are preparing ourselves for Holy Communion. "*Lord, I am not worthy*", you repeat, beating your breast and at the same time you go up to the rails. Like Simon Peter, and much more so, we are sinners. Our Lord would have plenty of reasons for leaving us alone, except for this : He came to call sinners in order to save them. Where would we go, poor sinners, if not to Him Who frees us from our sins ?

The Master replies to the very humble love of His disciple, reassuring Him. "*Do not be afraid* . . . . . All of a sudden you are no longer afraid to go and throw out your net once again in spite of our fatigue, in spite of the strain I put on your faith in commanding you to do something which quite reasonably seemed to you to be silly. Why should you be dismayed when I have repaid your confidence ? You believed in Me, I believe in you.

"Leave you alone ? But I want to attach Myself to you more than ever. You are a sinner. I know it. But this is what I need to free men from the empire of sin. I have need of helpers who know how to sympathise with the misfortunes of others because they have experienced them themselves .[1] Do not be afraid, to-day's miracle is only a beginning, the symbol, the gauge of other more marvellous catches for which I am planning your destiny. *From now on thou shalt be a fisher of men*".

Simon Peter does not demand any more precise explanation of these quite enigmatic words : "*fisher of men*". Simon is very doubtful of what the Lord means. Is he not himself caught completely at this moment by Jesus ? Caught to the point of not wanting to be let go ever. Caught in his youth and for the rest

---
[1] Heb., V. 2.

of his life.

" *Come and follow Me. I will make you into fishers of men* ". Jesus does not have to say any more. Simon and his fellow fishermen, Andrew, James and John, brought their boats into the shore, left their nets there and " *leaving all, they followed Him* ".

They left everything, their country, their family, the trade that kept them alive. These total decisions are not usually the result of long deliberations : they are as instantaneous as the grace that gives rise to them.

They left all to follow Him . . . Cynics, who are often also hair-splitters, give themselves the mediocre satisfaction of observing that, after all, the disciples did not give up a lot. They were ordinary folk who did not renounce great riches by leaving their boats, their nets and their cottages . . .

And what, even if they had possessed less still ! It is not *quantity* that gives the full measure of a sacrifice, but *totality*. Don't let us judge with the mentality of a treasurer of philanthropic society for whom generous gifts are the important sums, as opposed to the tiny contributions of small subscribers. Being generous does not consist in giving a lot, but in giving all one has. He who, in giving a little, gives up all he possesses is more generous than he who gives much while still keeping something for himself. The Master will confirm this later when He admires the poor widow, who pays into the Temple treasury the two mites that are all she has.

The four disciples do not imagine, at the moment, that they are making a considerable sacrifice. Loyally, they respond whole-heartedly to grace ; Jesus caught them, living ; they handed themselves over completely. Soon they themselves will be capable of catching men.

Simon cannot yet know that the day he begins to preach the Gospel, the first cast of his net will be no

less astounding than that in Lake Tiberias. When, on
the evening of Pentecost, the Eleven take a count of the
men whom they have baptised in the name of Jesus
Christ, the number of disciples shall have grown by
about three thousand persons. During the months that
follow this miraculous draught, the rhythm of conversions
will continue in a less extraordinary but uninterrupted
fashion. It will no longer be necessary for the Holy
Ghost to manifest Himself by exterior marvels ; it is
inside hearts that He will act. Piety, disinterestedness,
mutual kindness, of which the first disciples will give
such an example, will draw popular favour to them.
The historian of the Acts of the Apostles has kept witness[1]
of this for us. " And each day the Lord added to their
fellowship others that were to be saved ".

Peter knew, therefore, what it meant to catch men.
Let us examine with him, Brethren, what the task of
the apostle consists of.

It is not for our advantage alone that Jesus has asked
us for our life, and that we have given ourselves to Him
without reserve. " A Christian ", said Abbé Perreyve,
" is a man to whom Jesus Christ has confided all men ".
Every Christian who understands the privileges and
responsibilities of his baptism ought to continue the
work of Jesus Christ and win men over to the kingdom
of God. As he himself has been caught by Christ, he
ought, himself, in his turn, catch men who were living
in ignorance of their divine destiny, victims of error or
of sin. God wants to save them but He will not save
them unless we, the baptised, go to the help of those
whom He has placed around us.

There can be no doubt that here we are in the presence
of a grave obligation. To accept that among the people
around us in our life, on our very door-step, even in

*   *   *   *

[1] Acts. II, 47.

our own family perhaps, there are souls who remain strangers to the Gospel, is quite impossible to the Christian once he is conscious of his union with Christ. To say that one could go about winning one's own salvation happily, while beside one souls are going astray and about to be lost, is an unbearable sorrow for a Christian who loves Jesus Christ. The order in the parable stabs at us without respite. " Go out into the streets and the lanes of the city ; bring in the poor, the cripples, the blind and the lame. Go out into the highways and the hedgerows, and give them no choice but to come in so that My House may be filled ".

Our duty is clear, but many are slow to fulfil it because they think themselves unfit, little qualified or without sufficient authority . . . " *Homo peccator sum !* " I am not superior to those whom I ought to convince : neither in intellectual worth, nor in moral worth . . .

This hesitation will soon disappear if we tell ourselves what exactly Jesus meant by " fisher of men ". The lake fishermen had no other share in the miracle than an increase of tiredness : besides, their trouble was not lessened. Nevertheless, if they had thrown their nets into a good spot they would not have drawn out that shoal of fish themselves. In the same way, when St. Peter preaches and baptises all day on Pentecost, an Other than he has determined the conversion of his listeners. " You were converted before you saw me, merely because you were looking for me ", wrote Fr. Lacordaire to one of his new spiritual sons,[1] When a priest hears the confession of a long life of sin or the confidence of an unbeliever who wants to get instruction, it is God who has brought these two men to Him. And nonetheless God needs him, God uses him, his word,

---

[1] *Lettres à des Jeunes Gens,* p. 118.

his ministry to establish between the visitor and the priest the bond which will make the conversion easier. We are not worth anything and at the same time we are indispensable.

This rule is constant in the practise of the apostolate. " *Everything is done by God, and nothing is done without us* ". From which it follows that a Christian ought not to excuse himself out of humility, nor allege his insufficiency in order to abstain from apostolic action. God asks us not to spare our pains, to row, to throw out the net like the Apostles on Lake Tiberias. The rest is up to Him. The apostle will even have a better chance of aiding the divine work if, like Simon Peter, he is conscious of all that he lacks.

To catch men does not mean to draw them to oneself or to impose oneself on them, but to bring them back from error or from sin in order to lead them to God. Don't let us confuse the apostolate with simple proselytism. The need to proselytise is innate in each of us, it is not enough for us to admire, we want to share our admiration. What joy it is for a man to win a new recruit to his doctrines, to enrole a new partisan in his cause ! He would find out that if the whole world were suddenly, at one blow, converted to his ideas he would no longer be happy. Action exercised personally on one individual is so exciting ! Of all the victories that a man can win, this is the one of which he is most proud ; that another should adopt an opinion that he himself holds to be true.

Now, this is not the Christian apostolate. The apostle's ambition is very different and much higher. He is not looking for a personal triumph, but for the triumph of Christ. What we want to communicate to our brothers is not our own point of view, but a belief that we *know* to be true, because it is the word of God.

" *Thou shalt be a fisher of men* ", of living men ; that

is to say, of men so fully alive, in the full exercise of their liberty, that they can lead a higher and more fruitful life. It is not a question of forcing them to see things in our way, but of presenting the truth to them so that they adhere to it spontaneously, with conviction, with joy. To bully souls, to enroll them by force would be to wish to offer God corpses, not living men. At the least, this is to intend to paralyse souls and such a pretension is illusory. The bound conscience frees itself sooner or later and turns against that which chained it. " There is no plant which my Heavenly Father has not planted but will be rooted up ".[1]

We will not expose those who have confided in us their immense deception of only finding at the end of their researches a limited human wisdom, a human virtue with its weaknesses, when they were hoping to find Truth and Holiness. We will " catch " men, but only to give them to God. That is the Apostolate !

Since the apostolate, to be efficacious, implies the effacement of the apostle, our insufficiency is no longer an excuse. We will not let ourselves be dismayed by our natural deficiencies, above all, if we correct them, like Simon Peter, through a boundless affection for Our Lord.

In order to speak well of Jesus, one need only love Him. When one really loves Our Lord, one may not always find the reply to every question of the doubter, but one furnishes him with an argument which he was not expecting and which makes him reflect. Would Jesus be loved as much as He is, if He had only been a man like us ?

In order to turn a sinner from his irregular conduct, my Brethren, do not think that it is necessary that you should never have offended God yourself : remorse will creep more surely into his heart if he sees the efforts

---

[1] Matt., XV, 13.

that you accomplish so as not to lose, any more, the grace that Jesus's forgiveness gave you. You will raise men's courage again, without knowing it, simply because you learned, in your intimacy with Our Lord, strength to smile in difficulties, calm in contradiction, serenity in your distresses.

You do not expect, of course, that conversions will follow one another non-stop around you. Before " being taken alive ", men will struggle, but your patience will disarm them at length. It is possible that they will make you suffer, that they will prove themselves hard, supercilious and even evilly-disposed, but redemption only operates by means of sacrifice.

You will catch men. Not in the snares of a dialectic that arouses retorts, nor in an eloquence whose impression will be forgotten to-morrow ; not by the charm of a natural sympathy that can disappear as rapidly as it is born. You will catch them by what Christ has put in you, by what He has made of you. You will draw them by the influence of a virtue that is always careful to hide itself. You will win them by a charity which forces itself to be discreet. You will convince them by something that you do not realise yourself, I mean, the unconscious shining of your inner life, of your supernatural life. The most persuasive apostle will always be he who does not think of himself as such.

Think of all the men around us who need Jesus Christ ! The Holy Father repeats it periodically, that the instability of the peace, social conflicts, economic disorders, the confusion of souls, all these sufferings of our times can be remedied provisionally, partially, by legislative measures, treaties or protocol, but these are only palliatives. The evils of our society will only be cured by the reform of hearts, by the reign of Christ.

To make Jesus Christ reign, that is the task that falls to the lot of Christians in our time, a task as magnificent as it is formidable, and before which we feel ourselves much smaller still than Simon Peter must have felt himself when he began to evangelise the world. But the miracles of olden times will repeat themselves, men will come or return to Christianity if we, Catholics, with as much piety as humility, let Jesus Christ live fully in us, if we practice the law of the Gospel utterly.

CHAPTER IV

THE FAITH OF THE APOSTLE MUST NOT HESITATE

Why didst thou hesitate, man of little faith ?
(Matt., XIV, 31)

IT was not a year since Peter had left everything to follow Jesus . . . Since then what had he not received from the Master, what had he not learned from Him ? All the Saviour's actions, every word He pronounced in public, those He addressed to the carefully chosen little band of Apostles (for in the interval He had solemnly picked out the future chiefs of His Church, and Peter had been named as the leader of them)—even more so the influence that He exercised on the privileged twelve admitted to His intimacy at every moment : all that left a profound impression on St. Peter, we imagine, but the Gospel had no need to let us know it.

The first episode in which the sacred history brings Simon Peter back to our notice happens once again on the sea of Tiberias.

The Saviour has just multiplied the bread which the Apostles distributed to several thousand people. Astounded, the crowd wants to bear Him off in triumph to Jerusalem and proclaim Him king. The people still do not understand the exclusively religious character of His mission—and anyway, they will never be able to accept it. Also, to escape from their ovations, Jesus orders the Apostles to go on board immediately and to cross over to the other side of the lake. He will join them shortly. Then, having sent the crowd home, He retires to a hill, all alone, to pray.

Meanwhile, a contrary wind rises up and begins to blow violently upon the waters ; the waves hurl the boat backwards. The Apostles can no longer steer : when night falls, they are still in the middle of the lake. What can you do in such a storm, except to keep your position and wait for the wind to die down ?

It was shortly before the feast of the Pasch ; therefore, there was a full moon. From the hill, Jesus could follow the desperate efforts of the navigators. Then, at about three o'clock in the morning, before day-break, the Apostles think they see something that looks like a man, advancing towards them over the waves. The human shape of the apparition becomes more clear, but appears to pass them out. Trembling with fear, they shriek : " *It is a ghost* ". But Jesus speaks to them immediately to banish their fear : " *Take courage, it is Myself. Do not be afraid* ".

Then Peter, the impulsive one, makes this strange request : " *Lord, if it is thyself, bid me come to thee over the water* ". Why have some people emphasised what might be presumptuous in this prayer ? One should rather picture to oneself the state of soul of these men, overwhelmed already by the miracle of the multiplied loaves, then shaken by the storm for hours that seemed endless to them. What they see upsets them. The silhouette of their Master on the lake—then His voice which they recognised easily . . . What is this new marvel ? Surely it is He, it can only be He. He is, without doubt, going to calm the tempest . . . " Lord, is it You ? ", cries Peter, " Since it is You, let me join You ! " Do not let us suppose that he is looking for a miracle for his own benefit. He does not aim so high. It is only that his love makes him want to be near his Master immediately, as soon as possible. And Jesus knows that Peter is only obeying his ever-loving and prompt nature. If He had detected any mental reservations of distrust or any kind of desire to show off, He would not have replied as He did : " *Come* ".

Peter does not have to be told twice. He leaps out of the boat and walks in his turn on the water on his way to Jesus. Suddenly, the wind blows with increased rage. Seized by fear, the Apostle feels his heart falling, he goes under, he is drowning ! " *Lord, save me !* "

Jesus is already beside Him, He stretches out His hand, and brings him up to the surface. Meanwhile, the Saviour does not reproach him for his thoughtless demand ; He would reprove him sooner for having reflected too much, for having reflected when it was too late, when it was useless. In the presence of mystery, man is dismayed. Peter had not thought at first that he was asking for the laws of nature to be broken ; then he suddenly reflected that it was not normal to walk on water, that the wind would surely knock him down, and at that moment, fear seized him. He realised that he had given way to an insane desire. Doubt laid hold of him immediately and he sank . . . Jesus did not reproach him with his temerity. He only reproached him with one thing, to have supposed a quarter of a second after He allowed him to expose himself to danger that He would abandon him to it. " *Why didst thou hesitate, man of little faith ?* " Can one doubt Christ's love ?

Modicae fidei ! St. Peter's faith insufficient ? When it seems so great in comparison with our own ! Our faith will never be subjected to such a trial, and whatever our confidence in God, it is hardly probable that we will entreat Him for a favour of this sort. As well as that the lesson that this Gospel narrative holds for us does not consist of that. The lesson is of value for us on the single point of Peter's example concerning us. The Apostle's faith is truly that of which Jesus spoke on another occasion, the faith that moves mountains, that faces obstacles . . . It was only not lasting. *Modicae fidei :* man whose faith did not last, why did you hesitate ?

Do we not find our own inconstancy in these sharp changes of attitude on the part of Peter, first wildly enthusiastic and brave to the point of forgetting the most elementary prudence—then, the following moment, terrified by what he has dared to undertake and losing heart in face of the difficulty ?

Our faith, even more than his, has its ups and downs which are not the least test of our religious life : sometimes a spirit that is too mobile imagines that it sees its belief declining, sometimes confidence in God seems to founder all of a sudden. Theoretical or practical doubts, inconstancy of spirit or of will constitute so many obstacles to the accomplishment of our Christian vocation. And certainly we could avoid them, or, at least, we could surmount them instantly. Near the Saviour our faith must not hesitate.

* * * *

Brethren, you would like to possess a faith that remains always constant. Now, at certain times, you say, the truths of dogma present themselves to your spirit in a light that wins over conviction invincibly, and some other times your beautiful certitude is suddenly shattered. Insidious question marks appear around your dearest beliefs. Nothing seems proven to you any more. You want to believe always, but you do not dare say any more : " I believe ! "

What you ought to say in such a case, and with the same promptitude, is the prayer that saved Simon Peter : *Domine, salvum me fac !* Lord, save me !—But do not forget to go back over what happened immediately, for there is never anything without a cause. Why did you suddenly pass from serene and joyous faith to the torments of doubt ?

For divers reasons, but all of which lead back to this one, that you gave ear to other voices than that of Jesus Christ. The more you pray to Him, the more you look at Him, the more you listen to Him, the less the most impressive arguments of disbelief can have any effect on you. On the other hand, the most insignificant objections hold you up, once God occupies a lesser place in your life. Simon Peter did not hesitate to throw himself on the waters of the lake ; he only listened then to Jesus's word, " Come ". But as soon as he listened to the noise of the wind he faltered.

I do not forget, brethren, that the darkening of religious truths can take place without there being any fault on our part. Then it is just the means that God uses to purify our faith, still too attached to the need for tangible evidence, in order to make it stronger, more supernatural, more meritorious. The believer subjected to this temporary darkness, vigorously throws thoughts of doubt aside and though he can still see nothing, he repeats sadly : " Lord, I believe ! "

This is not the case of the man, who, on the contrary, fully makes up his mind to doubt the truths of faith. The night, into which he is plunged, springs unquestionably from negligence or imprudence, for which he himself is responsible. " One cannot *lose* the faith except through one's own fault ", wrote Mgr. d'Hulst about Renan. " The hypothesis that a soul, which *adhered sincerely* to the Christian religion, and which, without ever lacking integrity, faithfulness, disinterestedness, courage, without neglecting the voice of prayer in times of trouble, without listening to the suggestions of pride or of the senses, could be drawn by purely scientific motives into the abandonment of belief, such an hypothesis is incompatible with the truths of dogma, with the justice and goodness of God ".[1]

From the moment that a believer can no longer see clearly in matters of faith, let him observe himself closely. It will not be long before he discovers that, for

---

[1] Mgr. d'Hulst, *Mélanges,* vol. II, p. 332.

some time, his life of piety has been suffering a relapse,
that his prayers were said more rarely or less attentively,
that he was less severe on himself. Did not that sin
return, the gravity of which he knowingly made little
of ? If he does not yield to one of his evil passions,
certainly he does not repress them with the same vigour
as before. Resentment felt against someone else, a
question of interest where our probity is not absolute,
a too absorbing friendship, the awakening of baser
instincts that we do not stamp out quickly enough ; no
more is needed for the clouds to slip between God and
ourselves. And faith is weakened.

Quare dubitasti ? You only make the shadows greater
if you give doubt time to take shape. The fact that
difficulties in believing exist does not, in itself, create
a big problem. They exist, dearly beloved, even when
they do not bother you. Study and reflection ought
to be clarifying our religion all the time. But the truth
also exists when you do not see it, it exists as much as
when you see it, it has not changed since the day when
you first adhered to it, it does not change with your
fears, your desires or your faults. Your eyes were able
to see it as long as the habit of sin did not blind you.
Therefore, rip open the veils that hide it from you :
Domine, salvum me fac ! . . . Call for the Lord's help,
He will quickly stretch out His hand to you.

*   *   *   *

Much more than the fickleness of the spirit, the
inconstancy of our will exposes us to shipwreck. The
most damaging thing for the progress of our moral life
as for the efficacy of our apostolic action is not to founder
before a difficulty or even to retreat, dismayed by the
prospect of accepted sacrifice (in such a case, one can
correct oneself and make a new attempt) ; the critical
hour is not when the will bends, it is when it withdraws.

Quare dubitasti ? A moment ago, before the theoretical doubt, the spirit asked : Is it true ? Now before the *practical* doubt the will hesitates : *Is it possible ?*

We always enjoy beginning a new enterprise, its novelty enchants us. But when it comes to continuing, to repeating the same monotonous task, the will grows tired very quickly. To throw oneself into the battle, to overcome the first obstacles is somehow intoxicating, but to hold on to the conquered territory, to resist attacks, to stand up under onsets ! You cannot advance any further, you must content yourself with not retreating, that is what uses up courage quickly. After the enthusiasm of beginnings that gave every hope of progress, comes a depressing doubt as to the efficacy of your efforts. And often the worst is over before one gives in to discouragement. Everything is put in question. The pros and contras are weighed. One Christian has doubts about his salvation, another about his vocation, this man doubts if he can ever perform his duty, another does not know any more whether the task which he has undertaken is really the one that God assigned to him. They wonder if they have not taken too much on themselves, if they have not overshot the mark in believing themselves called to so high a virtue, or in proposing themselves for a work, for an apostolic labour that demands energy and perseverance beyond the ordinary.

It is a delicate business to choose one's duty oneself or to wish for more than others . . . Peter may well have thought this while he was struggling among the waves . . .

Modicae fidei. Our trust is too weak, I mean our trust in God. Since Our Lord calls—or merely because He allows us to come, *why should we doubt ?* It is inevitable that our will should get tired. It is a human will, limited, fragile and, at times, contradictory. We shall destroy it entirely if we stare into the gulf, or if we listen to the storms. We must look at Jesus. " *Let us fix our eyes on Jesus* ", St. Paul says to us, " *And run, with all endurance, the race for which we are entered* "[1]. Our fears for the future are based, no doubt, on plausible reasons or rather on the facts of experience, experience of our failures, consciousness of our weakness, certainty as to the difficulties to be surmounted. Simon Peter does not reason otherwise when the waters of the lake are about to swallow him. Since when has a lake been a highway ? . . . But he had been going beautifully across the waves when he only listened to Jesus's call.

And so with us, we will always find arguments to excuse our stops and our retreats. Why then don't we ground our hope in our confidence in the call of Christ, in the help of His grace ? Invisible realities, realities none the less ! We should like to be able to estimate exactly the resources with which we shall tackle to-morrow's task : humanly, nothing is more reasonable. In business, you never get involved unless you have your capital properly invested.

But in the great business of our sanctification, in the vaster business still of the salvation of the world, we must pledge ourselves without this security. The risks are not covered, we must set out with the smallest possible share of funds. God undertakes to increase our treasure every day—" for ", wrote St. Paul, " both the will to do it and the accomplishment of that will are something which God accomplishes in you, to carry out his loving purpose " [2] All the same, we shall not dare say that our desires for progress or for apostolate came from ourselves. Would we, of ourselves, have had the initiative to adapt ourselves to rigorous precepts, to discipline our independence, to master our passions when it would be so agreeable to give in to them ? Of ourselves,

---

[1] Heb., XII, 1–2.
[2] Phil., II, 13.

would we have consecrated our lives to God's reign? Would we have devoted ourselves to happiness and salvation? These aspirations of our souls bear the mark of Him Who suggested them to us. God, Who inspired us with them, helps us to realise them. On the lake, Jesus does not command the waves to be calm, just in order to show Peter that it was not the fury of the wind but his own lack of faith which had put him in danger. (St. John Chrysostom).

Don't let us be taken by the difficulties ; let us look, Brethren, at Him, Who calls us there, who lets us come there and who is capable of drawing us out of there. Don't let us start reasoning when we need to continue acting ; instead of discussing and trembling, quickly, let us start praying.

Let us repeat the short ardent supplication of the great Apostle : " Lord, save me ! " Let us invoke Jesus when we are distressed and weary. If He does not deliver us immediately don't let us suppose that He has forgotten us. He wants us first not to forget His presence. Let us renew our appeal without doubting for an instant that He loves us and His helping hand will keep us from foundering.

CHAPTER V

THE FAITH OF THE APOSTLE AND THE DESERTION OF THE MULTITUDE

Lord, to whom should we go ? Thy words are the words of eternal life.

(John, VI, 69)

SOME hours after Peter had walked upon the water, we find our Lord in the Synagogue at Capharnaum. The instruction that He gave there is one of the most moving pages of the fourth Gospel. Jesus draws the lesson of yesterday's miracle. He who multiplied the bread is Himself the new manna that God sends them. Living Bread descended from Heaven to give life to the world, He will be the divine food of our souls.

Then just as the crowd was carried away by the prodigy of the bread that was multiplied, so the audience at Capharnaum kicks against the unheard-of affirmations of the Saviour. His sermon is punctuated by interruptions, murmurings and protestations. The spiritual import of His words escaped the majority who finally revolt at the idea (the only one they grasp) that Jesus wants them to eat His flesh. " *This is strange talk* ", they say, " *who can be expected to listen to it ?* ". " *After this, many of His disciples went back to their old ways and walked no more in His company* ".

This must have been a dramatic moment, for it was not a question of a few isolated desertions, but a massive desertion ; *multi discipulorum ejus abierunt*. Without hatred, without threats, simply under the blow of an insurmountable deception, a great number of His disciples refuse to believe in Him. His words are too hard.

Note well the quality of those who left Him. They were not chance listeners who went away, shaking their heads or shrugging their shoulders, but disciples. These men had believed in Jesus, they had undergone the influence of His doctrine and His person, but from now on the charm is broken . . .

They had made sacrifices to come and follow Him, their renunciations were to no avail. They lose everything they have gained and everything they could yet gain. They compromised themselves for His sake by ranking themselves among His followers ; they had incurred the criticism of others. Now they pass over to the ranks of the others and go to swell the number of His detractors and His enemies.

While the group of deserters are retiring, the eyes of the faithful disciples are fixed on Jesus. Will the Master not call the malcontents back ? Will the Saviour make no attempt to prevent them leaving the way of salvation ? Is he no longer the Good Shepherd, who leaves his flocks and runs to look for the one sheep that has strayed until he has found it ? That day, the flock split up and scattered before an unyielding shepherd . . . Jesus let them go. This is a strange crowd leader, who is not interested in popularity.

We recognise here the perfect loyalty of Our Lord. He takes nobody on unexpectedly ; you cannot become a follower of His except with your eyes open. He does not hide the difficulties of the " narrow path " along which He leads us. Jesus only wants those who want Him. His yoke is sweet and His burden light but He does not promise a yoke which will not bind at all, or a burden that will weigh nothing. They will become sweet and light to people who accept them freely through love of Him. As for those who come to Him by force, or who follow Him cursing, they will find in Christianity neither joy nor ease but only a burden and a yoke.

This is why Jesus lets the disciples go, whom His speech disturbs. He must be known and taken as He is. He must be accepted with all His demands. We must either give Him the first place in our affections that He asks for or else there is nothing more for us to do but to leave Him.

Added to that, not only does the Saviour not try to keep up the number of His disciples but instantly he turns to those who had not wavered. He calls on the Twelve especially : " *Would you, too, go away ?* " Those who stayed with Him, did they do it from conviction, or only because they did not want to cause Him pain ? Jesus gives them their freedom : " Do not remain as My disciples if your feel any regrets or doubts in yourselves ".

Jesus does not use the words of thanks that they heard yesterday : " *You are the men who have kept to my side in my hour of trial* . . . " [1] He does not bolt the door to check the exodus ; on the contrary, He leaves it wide open. " You can go as well if you find my teachings too hard ". Jesus only wants people who are willing, convinced and decided as disciples. He will say to them immediately afterwards : " *Have I not chosen all twelve of you ?* " He chose them after a night of prayer, after weighing the value, disposition and aptitude of each of them. He chose them but He is ready to see them desert Him.

The Master who chose us before we knew Him intends us to choose Him freely in our turn. Chose, He says, between the majority and Myself, your instincts and My Gospel, the love of self and charity, egoism and justice, the broad highroad of desires or the " narrow path " of duty.

" *Would you, too, go away ?* " It was Simon Peter who replied in the name of the Twelve : " *Lord, to whom*

[1] Luke, XXII, 28.

should we go ? Thy words are the words of eternal life ".

The Apostle's reply jumps out quickly, ardently as usual. It is loyal as was the Saviour's question. They remain because they have no place else to go. " Where should we go, if we left you ? "

Peter does not think of choosing other masters, he does not think either that one can do without a master. He has no illusions about the urge to independence on which so many men falsely base their greatness. Not to obey anyone, to be one's own master, these claims of one's pride cannot fool a spirit that reflects. In reality, we all need a master, we all put masters over ourselves, the whole thing is to choose them well.

The person who thinks he is his own master, in fact obeys his passions. The man who throws off the yoke of divine authority bases his revolt on the authority of human advice. Those who rise up against their lawful masters are giving themselves over to mob-rule. They are " scared stiff" of what so-and-so may say about them, they howl with the wolves. The man, who makes the loftiest protests against the guardianship of religion, is enslaving himself, without knowing it, to other masters unworthy of a free spirit. His master is an opinion, a book, a companion, class interest or most tyrannical of all, his own ever-insatiable lust.

Simon Peter wanted a master for himself who would instruct him and elevate him. He wanted a leader to defend him and guide him. But who was there other than Jesus Who could teach him or lead him ? Who was there more worthy of his trust ? *Verba vitae aeternae habes !*

His words are hard, certainly, Peter does not deny it. It is remarkable, however, that this schism among the disciples was caused not by one of the severest of the Master's sermons.

For, later, Jesus will speak of the vital renunciations,

of the daily cross, and His followers will not wince at all.
However, these are words that will be " hard " in a
different way, hard to practise.

Yes, hard to practise but not so hard to understand.
The people at Capharnaum broke with the Saviour
on a question of doctrine, not of practice. It was not
the weakness of the flesh that made them revolt against
Him but their spirits' pride. They went away because
they could not admit that Jesus, their fellow-man, had
the power to give them eternal life, and by such unheard-
of means ; to give them Himself to eat. " *This is
strange talk, who can be expected to listen to it ?* "

But those who remain, those who believe in the doctrine
of the Eucharist, can " listen ", without their faith
failing, even to the harder lessons of the " narrow path "
and the ear of grain that will fructify only by dying.
Those who believe in the bread of life are no longer
afraid to die themselves.

Peter does not deny that Jesus' words are hard to
hear, but, at least, they do not lessen in any way the
person who accepts them ; they release him, they make
him greater. They are hard but they ennoble our poor
human lives. *Verba vitae!* Jesus's words help life.

Other masters flatter their disciples, they offer a more
comfortable morality, but without ever giving them
any certitude. Christ's doctrine affirms, makes certain ;
it is austere, cutting like a sword, but no other can equal
it in grandeur or fruitfulness. There is something eternal
in the Saviour's words. *Verba vitae aeternae habes.* " You
speak the final words that make one live for ever ".
The Saviour makes known to us and proposes to us the
*divine life that will transform our lives in uniting us eternally
to God.* It is the living and eternal God, Who speaks
through His mouth : " *To whom should we go ?* "

*   *   *   *

Let us re-read this page of the Gospel now, Brethren, thinking both of those of our kind, who have deserted Christ and of ourselves who intend to remain faithful to Him. That spontaneous cry of Simon Peter's was needed to scatter the terrible sadness that weighs on this episode of Jesus's ministry. How sincere our Evangelists are ! Nothing resembles a partisan work less than their brief resumés. A few words are sufficient for them to describe the admiration and enthusiasm that their Master aroused. But far from covering up any opposition, on the contrary, with relentless objectivity, they do not leave a single detail to our imagination when it comes to describing the rebuffs that He endured, the hostility He met with, the frightful treatment meted out to Him.

Of all the tests that Jesus had to undergo, the most cruel must have been, without doubt, the desertion of so many disciples. We would like to hope that the departure of all these people at Capharnaum was not final. St. John tells us, it is true, they " *walked no more in His company* ". Were there not several all the same, who returned to Him ? Who knows whether, after the Resurrection, at least, a few were converted by the Apostles' preaching ? Disciples ! Men, who had lived near Him ? Who had loved Him ! I seem to hear St. Paul exhorting them mildly. " Brethren, you acted in ignorance, repent then ! " [1] It seems impossible to me that they could all have forgotten Him and renounced Him for ever . . .

I must admit, however, that we know nothing about it and this is why the apostacy of so many disciples wrings my heart. I experience this same anguish acutely every Easter when in the joy of the numerous communions of the faithful (a joy usually made greater by the return to the altar of Christians who had not approached the sacraments for a long time) a disturbing sadness

---
[1] Acts, III. 17–19.

seizes me at the thought that, on the other hand, there are also Catholics, who every year, for the first time, do not fulfil their Easter duty. They have gone away, when will they return? Will they ever return? . . .

There are those who go off, without our knowing it, and there are those whom, as Jesus did, we must let go, for they cannot be with Him anymore. We see them going astray, powerless like the father of the Prodigal Son, and we can do nothing but wait for them and watch out for them from far off in order to offer the forgiveness of God to their wretchedness . . .

Jesus has announced it plainly to us in the parable of the Sower and the Seed. Perseverance is not the common lot of all the baptised, some fall away immediately, some after a few attempts at the Christian life. The most unfortunate are those whom the noon-day devil lays low and who desert Christ at the age when most of the prodigals have returned. A few go away, like those at Capharnaum, murmuring; they have, of course, to justify their conduct, " *Durus est hic sermo* ". Catholic doctrine, the latter say, with its categorical affirmations that exclude all evasions, no longer adapts itself to the evolution of our thought. It is no less absolute or intolerable for the former than is the rigorous Catholic morality which does not admit of any compromise with the unruly passions of the sinner.

They go off and their disconsolate parents or the most devoted of spouses, cannot hold them back. Often, in fact, brethren, when you foresee the spiritual drama which will unfold with the religious desertion of those you love, or when they themselves reveal it to you, then it is much too late for you to intervene with success. The break is already made.

But, perhaps, it is God, who allows your attempts to be unfruitful. Don't you believe that it would have been better for Judas to have accompanied the deserters at Capharnaum? Perhaps he would not have ended in despair.

Also, we are wrong to give in blindly to the magic of statistics. There are circumstances, where a number does not mean a victory but a defeat. The strength and vitality of the Church is not measured only by the extent of Her conquests. The integrity of Her doctrine, like the holiness of Her members, is brought about, at times, at the price of extremely painful but necessary exclusions and disagreements. The apostasy at Capharnaum was only, apparently, a check to Jesus' ministry. In reality, the Gospel was saved that day by the departure of those who could not remain. Now, it is not with a light heart that we see Christians going astray, whom it is impossible to keep with us. In renouncing Christ, they wound our souls and take a part of them away, but, beware, brethren, that their desertion does not damage your faith. There are apostacies that have overwhelmed the serenity of some believers. Let us recall to mind Jesus's sad prediction : It is inevitable that there should be scandals, and the words of St. Paul that echo Him : " It is inevitable that there should be heresies . . . " The Apostle states it even more precisely to his disciple Timothy : " We are expressly told by inspiration that, in later days, there will be some who abandon the faith ".[1]

Christians, do not let yourselves be impressed, especially you young people, by the spectacle of these brothers of yours who have abandoned our beliefs ! " What have they seen, these rare ' geniuses ' ", writes Bossuet in the funeral oration of Anne of Gonzaga, " What have they seen more than others ? How easy it would be to confound them, weak and presumptuous as they are, if it were not for the fact that they are afraid to take

---

[1] I Tim., IV, 1.

instruction. Do they think that they have seen the difficulties better than the others simply because they have given in to them, and that the others who have seen the same difficulties ignored them? Without taking it as high as the great Bishop had a right to do, be, at least, convinced, absolutely convinced, that a Christian capable of deserting Jesus Christ has never really known Him and never truly understood Him, even if the apostle had the rank of a Lamennais. If he had known Him, if he had understood Him, he would never have left Him. To whom can one go, in whom can one trust, once one has had Jesus for Master?

Whoever has truly understood Christ, has drawn from His words a light and strength which he can never renounce. Alas! They do not always protect one from passing weaknesses but they do prevent one from forgetting one's Saviour. For the Christian who has truly known Christ, the option presents itself in the form in which St. Peter proposes it to us: "*Lord, to whom should we go?*"

He must choose between Jesus and nothingness. If the Gospel is a lie, nothing is true. If the proofs of Christianity are false, no historical event can be proved. If the Gospel does not give us the true meaning of life, what are we doing down here? And who has played on us the rotten trick of putting us on this planet? If the charity that Jesus teaches us has not a divine origin and does not belong to God's eternal love, it is only a Utopia and a decoy, and it is the wrong-doers who are right. If Jesus was not God . . . Brethren, I will go no further, you feel an abyss would open under our feet.

Let us finish rather with Peter: "*Verba vitae aeternae habes*". To each of us (and this is what, as Christians, you will recognise if you have known and understood Him) to each of us, Jesus spoke the words that make us live for ever. Heaven came to explain this earth to us. The Son of God resolved the enigma of man. Christ came to add mercifully His divine life to your incompleted and unsatisfied human lives here below. Jesus gave us life which revives us, completes us and transfigures us ; life which unites us eternally to God.

CHAPTER VI

FAITH IN THE DIVINITY OF JESUS CHRIST

Thou art the Christ, the Son of the living God.
(Matt. XVI, 16).

FOLLOWING St. Peter we have become aware of the demands of our vocation as Christians, called personally to salvation and called to save the world. An admirable task, but one which implies constantly renewed efforts as well as a blind confidence in Our Lord, which alone is capable of correcting our weakness and of making us independent of the opinion of men.

Meanwhile our faith is not only a feeling of tender confidence in God. This sentiment rests in certainty of spirit. To believe is first of all, to adhere without reserve to the truth that Jesus has taught us. The episode of Peter's confession at Cesarea sets in relief some of the beliefs from which the Christian draws a particularly precious help, as much for his own sanctification as for his apostolic tasks. Faith in the divinity of Jesus, faith in the deification of the Christian, faith in the divinity of the Church, faith in the person of the Head of the Church, these four articles of Catholic dogma are now proposed for our meditation.

Peter's confession at Cesarea marks a decisive date in the religious history of humanity, I mean the divine foundation of the Church and the Papacy.

Everyone knows the solemn declaration that Our Lord made on this occasion. Plain enough to convince an unprepared reader, of its own accord, it impresses itself with more force still, when it is not separated from the words of Simon Peter to which it is a reply. So Peter's " confession " is a categorical affirmation of

the divinity of Jesus. So that here we listen to the first
teaching of him who is to be the first of the Roman
Pontiffs. May it not only affirm our own conviction
but penetrate it with the love that exalted the faith of
the great Apostle . . .

It is not without interest to note the spot where this
event took place. Look for Cesarea of Philippi on
the map of Palestine ; you will find in the North at
the extreme confines of Jewish territory, among a largely
pagan population. We are in fact at the stage when the
opposition declare themselves openly against Jesus.
His contemporaries were expecting a Messiah who would
restore the prestige of Israel and subdue the whole
world by force of arms. Instead of leading them to
the marvellous and easy victories to which they were
looking forward, Jesus invited them to the conquest of
themselves. His sermons are so many calls to the
practice of justice, of charity, of repentance and renunciation . . . . . Decidedly, His words were too hard.
The Master could not even speak openly, He had to
have recourse to the veiled language of parables.

To let the first waves of hostility die down, Jesus
left Galilee, disappointed by the infidelity of the towns
where he had worked His first miracles. " Woe to thee,
Chorozain, woe to thee, Bethsaida ! Woe to thee,
Capharnaum ! " He was going to profit from this
voluntary exile to complete the formation of the disciples
who had not abandoned Him, the Twelve, in particular.
And since people did not want to recognise His Messianic
character, He decided to reveal His true personality
to the faithful disciples.

He asks them, " *What do men say of the Son of Man ?* "
The disciples simply report what they have heard.
Many people had given credit to the rumour circulated
by Herod ; the latter, in the grip of remorse for having
let the Precursor be murdered, imagined that Jesus was

none other than John the Baptist resurrected and the rumour had spread. " *Some say John the Baptist* ". But other stories were going the rounds as well ; Jesus might be Elias, Jeremy or some other prophet, come back to earth. You will notice that no one suggested that He might be the Messiah.

When they had finished the Saviour asked them bluntly : " *And what of you ? Who do you say that I am ?* " As always, Simon Peter is the first to reply, " *Thou art the Christ* ", that is to say, " Thou art the Messiah ". His faith did not hesitate for a second, but now it brings him far beyond Jewish beliefs. The sermon at Caphar-naum opened numerous horizons to him. Jesus is the living bread come down from Heaven to give life to the world. It is not enough to see in Him the Messiah, the messenger of God, " *Thou art the Son of the living God* ", Jesus had given Himself the title that He liked best because it made Him closer to us, " Who do they say the *Son of Man* is ? " Peter awards Jesus the title that is His own, " Thou art the *Son of the true God* ".

It has been attempted, of course, to narrow the sense of Simon Peter's profession of faith. Did he not just mean to speak of a moral relationship in the sense in which the angels and some of the characters of the Old Testament were called " *sons of God* ", because they had been the object of a special mission or a special favour from the Most High. This interpretation does not fit in with Jesus' reply : *Blessed art thou, Simon son of Jona, it is not flesh and blood* ", that is to say it is not the natural lights of man, " *it is my Father in Heaven that has revealed this to thee* ".

If the expression, " Son of the living God ", had only been intended by Peter as a metaphor, he would not have needed any supernatural illumination. He could have found that much out for himself. But Jesus is certain that what the Apostle has just declared he could not have discovered on his own. What he, faithful like all the Jews to the dogma of the divine unity, has just said, God alone could have inspired. So Peter has properly affirmed the close, unique. connatural relationship which binds Jesus to the living God.

" None knows the Son truly except the Father and none knows the Father truly except the Son "[1].

It is because He is really Son of God that He possesses the exclusively divine power of remitting sins. On the other hand, His adversaries would not have persecuted him to the point of killing Him, if they had seen in Him only a false Messiah. " They could not forgive Him ", wrote St. John, " for making Himself equal to God, for making Himself God, being only a man " [2]. Caiaphas will not need witnesses to condemn Him. From the accused's own mouth he gets the " blasphemy " which will mean a verdict of death. " Art thou the Christ, the Son of the blessed God ? ". " I am ", replied Jesus.

" *Thou art the Son of the living God* ". Peter's words have the same rigorous significance. At the moment when men are turning away from the Son of Man, Peter, the future Head of the Church, he who must not waver, when it is a matter of expressing the truth, Peter, enlightened from on high, formulated the first act of total faith in the true God, who " became nothing " to put on our humanity.

Let us leave, Brethren, the fields and gardens that slope away in terraces above the fertile hills of Cesarea and return to our own times.

After nineteen centuries men still speak of Jesus. No other epoch has produced as vast a literature as has ours on the topic of Him. Almost every year, studies of the Gospel text and biographies of Christ appear ;

---

[1] Matt., XI, 27.
[2] John, V, 18 ; X, 33.

continually cleverer apologies follow one another on the most daring themes.

The question of Cesarea has never ceased to be the question of the hour. "What do men think of the Son of Man?" Men's opinions are always clashing. The boldness of the unbelievers has even passed the limits that one would think possible, but they have gone so far in their often puerile fantasies that they now cannot harm the serenity of the believers or the impassioned admiration of Christ's adorers.

What are they saying, these people around us, these people who are not of our sort? Some say, "Jesus is a thinker without equal, the most remarkable example of humanity,—but a man". Others, "He is the greatest of the revolutionaries, but the Church corrected His doctrine to safeguard the privileges of the powerful", for which some blame the Church, and many more rejoice. Others see in Him a dreamer whose fancies will never come to anything on our planet.

"But you, who do you say that I am?" Brethren, we repeat, do we not, Simon Peter's act of faith, with a certitude strengthened by the very attacks of which it is the object. Without going in detail into those direct proofs for the divinity of Jesus, which after all every Christian ought to know, I will confine myself to taking up what might be called an *impromptu argument,* drawn from the observation, pure and simple, of the personality of Christ and which is absolutely inexplicable if He is not God.

That people are still getting worked up about Jesus at the present day, should this not give food for thought to those souls, who see in Him only a man? In consequence of this *prejudice,* shouldn't one conclude that if anyone should never be mentioned after His death, it is the humble workman from Nazareth, who never held either a sword or a pen and who exercised no function in His country ? This poor carpenter thought He was the Messiah ! In a few months the authorities of this country would have set him right. Most of His followers had already left Him, when He disappeared from the scene under one of the fairly frequent condemnations of the age in which He lived.

And the young hero of that extremely local adventure, whose name should have been completely forgotten by the following century, took His place in history from the day after His death. Immediately, He occupies the central place in history. There is no name that human lips will pronounce so often as His ! There is no name against which such violent hatreds will rage ! Confucius, Mahommed are not hated ! Dead people are not hated, one only hates a living person. On the other hand, there is no name which can awake on earth more tenderness or more enthusiasm. And this name is supposed only to be that of a little joiner from a tiny village in Galilee at the time of the Roman occupation ! If anything is inexplicable, this surely is !

If we want only to find a strange paradox here, let us open the Gospel. On the hypothesis that Jesus is only a man, this book is quite incomprehensible and the character portrayed merits at the best only silence. What can one think, indeed, of this Jewish workman who puts Himself above kings and angels ? He changes the law of Moses ; the word, " I " is continually on his lips, " You have been told . . . but I say to you . . ! " " Heaven and earth will pass away ", he proclaims, " but my word will not pass away ! "

Did you note His demands ? He intends all men to embrace His doctrine and to consecrate their lives entirely to Him. One must love Him more than one's father and one's mother, be ready to sacrifice everything for Him, even life itself. Such ideas, if they are proposed by a man, could only come from a tyrant or a madman.

Imagine a saint, who would dare express himself like this ! Let us make a choice ; either Jesus is neither a superior man, because His words are devoid of wisdom, nor a saint because,—to say the least of it, He lacks humility,—or else He is a master of His thought, He is truthful, He is good (the rationalists do not raise any questions on this point) so that He really has got a right to the prerogatives and sacrifices that God alone can claim from us.

With a word Jesus changes water into wine, He commands the storm ; at His word the deaf hear, paralytics are cured, the blind see, the dead arise. Besides, notice how His miracles uniquely drew the crowds and grouped the devoted disciples around a thaumaturgy that has never been common with teachers When He commands the forces of Nature they obey His voice. His words are therefore efficacious. Then, just as He says to the dead " Arise ", He affirms quietly that He can remit sins, that He—no one else—will distribute to each person the reward or punishment that their earthly actions shall merit. Even more, He asserts that He will raise all men on the last day, that Heaven shall consist in being with Him and damnation in being separated from Him.

Once more, if the person who expresses Himself like this is only a man, why wasn't He once and for all fixed to the pillory ? What a mixture of pride and deceit in one human brain ! Meanwhile, His incomparable sanctity is unanimously admired and the marvellous beauty of His morality. Nobody suspects His sincerity. His generosity, His patience, His disinterested charity, all are commended without restriction !

Those who thought that they would simplify the problem of Jesus by deciding *a priori* that He must be only a man, from then on, are confronted by an in-coherent character, frankly outside the laws of humanity,

the least human man there is. To escape the obscurities
of the mystery of the Incarnation they have made of
Christ an indecipherable enigma.

Certainly the union of the two natures, divine and
human, resists analysis ; but it is the only explanation
that leaves to the person of Christ His perfect unity, all
His grandeur and all His human beauty.

*   *   *   *

If now we consider the problem as solved by confining
ourselves to the simple observation of facts, it must be
recognised that the dogma of the incarnation clears
up the mystery of Jesus immediately.

He has all man's natural infirmities. He is hungry
in the desert, He is thirsty at Jacob's well, He knows
tiredness, He is moved, troubled, He is sad, He weeps.
He experiences all our weaknesses, and at the same time
one cannot discover in Him any infirmities that bear
the mark of sin, neither those that lead to it, nor those
that spring from it ; neither ignorance, nor difficulties
with virtue, nor inclination to evil.

We suffer our infirmities ; He took on our weaknesses [1]
He knew poverty and hunger because He wanted to.
But when He wished, five loaves of barley bread were
enough to feed a crowd, and He found the money to
pay His taxes in the mouth of a fish.

Before Lazarus' tomb, He weeps. That is man.
Then, He invokes the Father who always listens to Him,
and still weeping He brings a man who has been dead
for four days back to life. That is God !

As God, He shone with glory on Thabor when He
conversed with Moses and Elias. As Man, He was
prostrated at Gethsemane and His brow was beaded

[1] See Monsabré, Carême 1879, *Les infirmités de Jésus-Christ ;* Mgr.
Besson, *L'Homme-Dieu,* 6e Conférence.

with drops of blood.

" My Father has greater power than I ", says He, because He is a man, but He also says, " My Father and I are one ", because He is God. [1]

He is pitiable during the Passion and just like all sufferers. At the same time, with one word, He can throw the men, who come to arrest Him, to the ground, and He heals the ear that has been sliced off. On the point of death, the Son of Man had given the cry of despair of every conquered person, but immediately the Son of God expires in the greatest peace : " Father, into Thy hands I commend my spirit ". Fastened to the Cross, He cannot come down from it, but when He gives His last sigh, the sky is darkened, the earth trembles, rocks are split open. So, from Bethlehem to Calvary the life of Jesus is full of continual contracts. Disconcerting and unintelligible, if Jesus is only a man, they harmonise wonderfully, the moment one recognises His divinity. It may be noticed that of those weaknesses of ours which belong to Him because He is really man, He borrows from us those He wants when He wants them, He casts them off when it pleases Him, because He is really God.

Jesus is as truly man as He is certainly God. Jesus is not a man who passed Himself off as God or a man who believed that He was God. (What a poor man they would make of Him, to think Him capable of such cunning or such silliness !) It is God who shows Himself as a man. Not a man who over-rates Himself, but God who has made Himself man.

Let us leave these constructors of systems in the quandary to which their conclusions have led them. Things have not changed since Jesus lived on earth. There is no middle way ; if one does not adore, a sad

[1] John, XIV, 28 : X, 30.

courage is needed to villify Him. Some moderns thought that they could escape this dilemma by denying His existence, and after all, this trick, crude as it is, and irreconcilable with the data of history goes less against common-sense than the distortions and falsifications that must be inflicted on the Gospel text in order to deny the divinity of Christ. Jesus must be accepted completely or denied completely.

We Christians are lucky who, knowing what He is and understanding Him fully, can, like St. Peter, adore in Him the Son of the living God.

CHAPTER VII

THE CHRISTIAN IS MADE GOD-LIKE THROUGH THE CHURCH.

And I tell thee this, in my turn, that thou art Peter, and it is upon this rock that I will build my Church.
(Matt. XVI., 18).

SIMON has confessed the divine sonship of Jesus. He certainly would not know how to elucidate all the mysteries that the union of the divine nature and the human nature in the person of Christ implies, but at least he is certain that in Jesus, God is united to our humanity, " Thou art the Son of the true God ".

Our Lord's reply is neither less mysterious nor less sublime, if one takes the trouble to penetrate its profound significance. " *And I,* (who have already named you Peter, Rock) *tell thee that thou art the rock upon which I will build my Church* ".

The connection that exists between the Master's words and those of the Apostle may not perhaps be at first apparent. Peter had introduced us into the inaccessible regions where the living God is. Jesus' metaphor seems to bring us down to earth immediately, where the divine builder proposes to raise an edifice of which Peter will be the foundation.

Now, the two confessions, that of St. Peter and that of Jesus, follow the same plan. Jesus' promise echoes the disciple's act of faith. Peter rendered glory to the Son of God who came to live among men and Jesus promises to men the glory of becoming in their turn sons of God, for this will be the privilege of those who are to be the members of the Church.

This is why, Brethren, before examining the primacy of St. Peter in the work of Christ—and besides to understand it better—we will apply ourselves to determining the exact notion of this institution that Jesus did not name without a precise intention, " *My Church* ".

*   *   *   *

The saints have inspirations that put them instantly in possession of truths to which others attain only after laborious researches. Thus, our little Joan of Arc, the object of snaring interrogations of the theologians eager to catch her out in flagrant heresy, foiled their manœuvres by this ingenuous declaration, " *It seems to me, God and the Church are all the one* ". In the simplicity of her faith she knew more about it than the teachers who were claiming to judge her. She said what was strictly true : " God and the Church are all the one ".

Such a formula astonishes some. If the Church claims a divine origin and constitution, they say, must one not admit that its life, its activity, its history bear an undeniably human stamp. All the same, one ought not impute to God the errors and the faults of the faithful and the Heads of the Church, and, for example, since we have referred to it, the unworthy trial of Joan of Arc. That God assists His Church is certain ; without that divine assistance she would not have lasted so long. But is it not too much to identify God and the Church ? " It seems to me, God and the Church are all the one ".

Meanwhile the Church continues the Incarnation in a real way. Jesus took care to underline this liaisom " As my Father has sent me ", He said, " so I also send you ". The same gesture by God which sent His Son down to a little corner of our earth is prolonged and spread out till the end of time. When Jesus was walking the roads of Palestine, He contained in Himself the whole Church ; since the Ascension, the Church contains Jesus completely. The Church is " Jesus freely and magnificently spread out in time, place and number " [1] The Church is " the permanent Incarnation of the Son of God " [2].

Outsiders can only recognise the Church by its exterior. They see in Her a school where Peter teaches thousands of disciples the unique doctrine of Christ ; or else a sort of army, in which the soldiers only have to obey the Heads, who are alone in charge of operations ; or sometimes an administration (it is imagined too often under this aspect) an administration, exercised by civil servants, which Christ has commissioned to serve men on carefully determined conditions.

Unhappily many Catholics go no farther than this extrinsic and incomplete view of the Church. They are heard to say : " The Church teaches, the Church orders, the Church forbids." When they speak of the Church they always think of the teaching Church or the hierarchical Church. But, you, Catholics, you are the Church ! You are " His Church ! " The Church is not only the Pope and the Bishops, it is really composed of all the baptised in whom Jesus Christ continues to live and whom He has made the children of God.

* * * *

Etymologically the name of the Church, Ecclesia, (ἐκκλησία) means the meeting of those called, " the assembly of those who have been called together " " Our Lord calls us to Him, ' Come, follow me '."

---

[1] Mgr. Gay, *Vie et vertus chrétiennes*, chap. XVII.
[2] Moehler, *Symbolique*, Book I, chap. V, § 36.

He summons us to communicate eternal life to us, that
is to say, His divine life, for eternal life is not that which
will come later, it is not our little human life prolonged
in the Beyond. Eternal Life is the very life of God that
we receive through Jesus Christ and which we possess
from now on.

He calls us to Him and He gives us His *doctrine* first
of all, so that *His thought* may become ours. " The man
who listens to my words . . . . the man who has faith in
me enjoys eternal life "[1]. The verb is not in the future,
the disciple, the believer *possesses* eternal life.

He calls us and He imposes *His commandments* so that
our will accords with His. " If thou hast a mind to enter
into life, keep the commandments " . . . " and he will
be true to my word and then he will win my Father's
love and we will both come to him and make our continual abode with him "[2]. Is that not already a type
of " incarnation " ? We will make our abode with
him . . .

His Church unites those whom Jesus calls to follow Him,
to imitate Him, to love Him, and with whom He
establishes an intimacy which alone defines the word
" communion " (χοινωνία), fellowship " exactly, a union
in which everything *is common between Him and us* ". The
God, who has called you into the fellowship of his Son,
Jesus Christ, our Lord[3].

To be a member of the Church, is just to be one with
Him.

At baptism, we are born to the divine life, that is to
say, the life that the Father gave to the world through
His Son and which is communicated to each of us by
the Holy Spirit. We should go on our knees to say

---

[1] John, V, 24 ; VI, 47.
[2] Matt., XIX, 17 ; John, XIV, 23.
[3] I Cor., I, 9.

this simple formula : In the name of the Father, and of the Son, and of the Holy Ghost ! It proclaims our union with the God-head. From that day there exists between Christ and the baptised person, as real and fruitful a union as that which joins the branches to the trunk of a tree, for Jesus is the vine and we are the branches. The vine-shoots have not just got a rough resemblance to the vine, they are *produced* by the vine. The vine-shoots are not attached to the vine in the same way that one fixes garlands to trees on the day of processions of the Blessed Sacrament ; the vine-shoots *share the life of the vine.* So the life of Jesus, the divine sap, passes into the souls of all those who make up His Church. It creates between Him and us all a *unity of life* for a *community of action.* " I am the vine and you are the branches ".

St. Paul finally pictures the Church as an organism which he calls the *body of Christ.* The Church is the new and eternal body of Jesus Christ. *Christus caput Ecclesiae* [1]. Jesus is the head, the head of the body of which all of us are members and of which the Holy Ghost is the soul. As the brain influences the body co-ordinating the different functions performed by the organs, so all the members of the mystical body depend closely and directly on Jesus who is its Head, and through Jesus they are ' jointly and severally responsible ' for each other. " And you are Christ's body, organs of it, depending on one another " [2]. The divine life of Jesus circulates in all the members of the mystical body. There is no body without a head, but the head alone does not constitute a body, so that the members of the Church are the necessary complement of Christ. The moral exhortations of St. Paul are usually bound up with this doctrine of the mystical body, that is why he comes back to it so

---

[1] Eph., V, 23.
[2] I Cor., XII, 27.

often. Who does not recall the familiar formulae of the Apostle? " Christ is wholly in all of us ! Jesus Christ is my life ! " Let there be no more talk of Jews or of Greeks, of slaves or of free-men. " You are all one person in Jesus Christ . . . From Christ and from you God has made a single new man ".

Thus the Church continues the Incarnation. Without doubt the union of God and man was personally realised in Jesus Christ, and this mystery is obviously not reproduced in each of us. What subsists of the Incarnation is the moral but real union of the Son of Man with all the members of His Church individually but conjointly. Jesus does not unite Himself solely with me, I am united to Him because I am a member of " His Church ", because I am a member of the body of which He is the head and remain joined to other members of that body. The Son of God has clothed Himself in a new collective humanity which is " His Church ".

St. Paul is not the inventor of the doctrine, Jesus pronounced still stronger words in the prayer with which He brought His visible mission among us to an end. He prayed then for His Church, for those whom the Father had confided to Him and for those, who in the apostle's phrase, are to find faith in Him, for us, in consequence,

> " Father, as Thou art in Me,
> And I in Thee,
> May they too be one in Us . . . "

He does not hesitate to repeat Himself, " that they should all be one, as we too are one ; that while thou art in Me, I may be in them and so they may be perfectly made one " [1]. This is His Church.

Through the members of His Church, the Son of God continues His work on earth ; He continues to pray, to advance the reign of His Father, to destroy

---

[1] John, XVII, 21, 23.

the reign of sin. He continues to preach, to love, to suffer. For example when Saul, the furious adversary of the Christians, is overthrown on the road to Damascus Our Lord says to him, " I am Jesus whom thou persecutest ". But Saul was not interested in Jesus, whom he had never known ; he was concerned with those Jews who were in the course of constituting a little schism in Israel among the most pious elements of the nation. However to persecute the Church is to persecute Jesus. Jesus and the Church are but one. " *I in them* ".

The Church is a divine and human brotherhood ; Jesus is a brother to each of us and through Him we are brothers to each other. The ties of brotherhood are not opposed to the hierarchy prescribed by the Saviour. St. Paul explains that not all the members of a body have an equal importance but this is not to diminish the value of the weakest members, they are on the contrary, the most necessary [1]. In the Church also, " the small, the obscure, those without position " are united directly to Christ as much as the visible heads whom they obey and all form with Him a single body.

*　　*　　*　　*

Let us savour at leisure all the joy that Catholics ought to feel knowing themselves to be so intimately united to Jesus Christ. St. Paul, when he gives himself up to it, does not know how to moderate it any more. *Jam non estis hospites et advenae.* We are no longer vagabonds on the earth, wandering without any aim ; in the eyes of God we are no longer homeless strangers in a supernatural world. *Sed estis cives sanctorum.* We are the fellow-citizens of the saints ; the chosen ones of Heaven have already arrived at that place to which we are making our way. *Domestici Dei.* We belong to

---

[1] I Cor., XII. 22.

the family of God, in God's household we are His sons [1].

It is through the Church, don't let us forget it, that we are united to the Saviour. Our intimacy with Him has for condition and corollary, a close communion of all Christians among themselves. The Church which deifies the individual, suppresses all individualism. The duty of all is to serve Jesus Christ together and to serve Jesus Christ in each of His members. The great man in the kingdom of Jesus ought to be the servant of His brethren. This is why Peter's successor is called the " servant of servants ".

Jesus lives in each of us, but He only comes to us if we are members of His mystical body. It is the Church which unites us to Him. It is the Church which gives us Jesus Christ. The Church, that is to say, the priest, who baptises us and gives us the help of the sacraments, the teaching of the Doctors which protects us from all error, the beneficent authority of the leaders, who guide and protect our liberty, but also the merits of all the martyrs, the example of all the saints, the prayers of all the just, the sacrifice of all who have been tested, the society of all our brethren, known or unknown, those to whom we have been good, those also who by their goodness or their severity, are to furnish us with innumerable occasions for a little daily step closer to sanctity. Let us be brought to Christ by the great current of divine life which circulates in His Church.

But our role ought not be restricted to receiving without ever giving. Encouraged by some, we ought in our turn to win over others. We cannot just be, in the mystical body, the paralysed and inert member that the whole body nourishes and serves while it does not participate in the common life. Let us keep a careful watch also lest we become the sick member who risks infecting all around him. The efforts that we

---
[1] Eph., II, 19.

make to release ourselves from sin will give health to the whole body. Our personal response to Jesus' influence will co-operate for the sanctification of the whole Church.

The weakest members are the most necessary. Do not let us lose sight, Brethren, of the considerable importance of the most humble of the faithful in the Church of Jesus Christ. In an army the value of its heads would be reduced to nothing without the good will, the discipline, and the courage of the soldiers ! And, in more than one case, the soldier's initiative decides the victory of the chief.

Now we often meet with this case in the Church. The *works* from which Catholicism draws a just pride have no doubt been approved by the heads of the Church but they are usually due to the virtue, the generosity, the sacrifices of the most humble children, who become through them Her most illustrious saints ; Francis of Assisi, Vincent de Paul, Jeanne Jugan, the first Little Sister of the Poor, Ozanam, John Bosco. Almost all the holy enterprises of the Church have started from below ! They have afterwards been controlled, modified, directed, encouraged by authority, but they were conceived and realised first of all by the " members who seemed to be the weakest ".

In the same way it is the Church of Rome and she alone who ought to lay down the regulations for the Christian cult, but these were two humble Christians Julienne du Mont-Cornillon who got the feast of Corpus Christi and Margaret Mary that of the Sacred Heart.

More rarely, but nonetheless sometimes, we can notice a similar phenomenon even in questions of dogma. In the Middle Ages, for example, the Doctors were still hesitating whether to pronounce on Our Lady's Immaculate Conception, when popular devotion had already advanced beyond the affirmative conclusions of the theologians.

We ought not therefore put too low a value on the position which we faithful occupy in this Church of which Peter is the head but of which we are the members. Peter could do nothing without us, no more than we could do anything without Peter. Let it be our heartfelt wish to be active members of the Church. Docile to the faith, certainly, but living the faith fully so as to increase it in others. Obedient to the directions of the Hierarchy, assuredly, but quick to understand their spirit and bold to put them into practice. Faithful in order to make ourselves holy, yes, indeed, but no less anxious to spread the holiness of Jesus Christ in the world.

We will never finish thanking the Saviour for having taken the bread of the Pascal supper in order to change it into the divine food of our souls, saying "This is My Body". He did not perform a lesser miracle when He created His Church, changing insufficient and sinful men such as ourselves into the mystical body by which He continues to be among us, always, till the end of the world. What are we Catholics? *Vos autem corpis Christi*. We are the body of Jesus Christ.

CHAPTER VIII

THE DIVINE PERPETUITY OF THE CHURCH.

Thou art Peter and it is upon this rock that I will build my Church ; and the gates of Hell shall not prevail against it.

(Matt. XVI, 18.)

THIS solemn promise of Our Lord's is grave and re-assuring at the same time. It binds Him who has pronounced it so that at the same time it constitutes a proof of the divinity of Christ and the certainty of the divinity of His Church.

For us, these two verities are blended because the Church is the body of Christ. But what man would ever dare to assert that his work will last for ever ? An institution capable of lasting for ever escapes human laws. As her founder was man and God, the Church is divine as well as human. In as much as she is human she shares in the imperfections of all the works of man ; but if at the same time she defies laws common to all human societies, one ought indeed to recognise a divine work in her.

Meanwhile Jesus' prediction contains an element the realisation of which ought to make the divinity of the Church even more obvious. The kingdom of God which the Saviour is founding on earth, will *last* when all human societies have faded away, and gone into decline, (and that is miraculous) but, even more so, this miracle will be accomplished *in spite of the continual assaults of the powers of Hell*. Pascal took careful note of this miraculous character of the perennity of the Church. " What is admirable, incomparable, and, wholly miraculous is that this religion which has lasted for ever has always been subject to attack. A thousand times, she has been on the brink of universal destruction and each time that she was in that state, God relieved her by an extraordinary stroke of His power ".

It occurs that Catholics let themselves be impressed by what seems too human in the Church, either in the past or in the present ; others are frightened of the future which holds a mostly pagan or repaganised world. How good it is therefore to remember Jesus' promise, the history of which is for us its faithful realisation.

Would open persecution or the underhand struggle be too much for us ? We know that it is not only against men's malice that the Church must defend herself in order to pursue her work of conquest. Jesus did not hide it from us : Sin will always rise up against the Church, the powers of evil will rage without respite against the kingdom of God. Why should we expect a tranquil rest which would be, without doubt, otherwise fatal to the virtue of Christians ? Our Lord warned us of the hatred of Hell, its violences and its cunning, its coaxing manœuvres and its murderous treacheries. But the infernal hostility will rage in vain, the Church of Christ, so justly called militant, will never be conquered. " *The gates of Hell shall not prevail against it* ".

* * * *

Without broaching here, Brethren, the subject of the naturally inexplicable conditions of what is called the Christian fact, (it would need much more discussion) that is to say, the very existence of the Church, let us limit ourselves to observing the response that nineteen centuries of Catholicism have made to the audacious prophecy of Christ.

How easy it was for the powers of Hell to destroy a society whose members were subjected to the limits and the weaknesses of human nature ! Their means are known to us and they have put them in to practice.

The first is *Money*. One cannot undertake anything without this indispensible lever. And still they were poor people who imposed Christianity on the Roman Empire. In every generation, besides, it was the apostles who were detached from riches who converted men to the Gospel.

While everywhere else the rich are using their influence to win themselves a clientèle, in the Church it is the poor who seduce the rich and the latter who give up their possessions to offer temples to God, hospitals to the sick, work and help to the poor. Hell understands nothing of this : it is the world turned upside down !

But Hell is cunning. Since the people of the Church are men, it will try to pervert them by love of money. The Church receives endowments, fortunes, domains. Her heads are like princes and enjoy the privileges of property. Hell has them ! No, for Jesus watches over His Church. At the opportune moment, with divine skill, He makes human laws come into play. The riches of monks and prelates, when they are no longer employed for the common good, arouse the envy of great and small. Periodically despoiled, the Church is brought back by the injustice of the spoliators to the simplicity of her origins, and Hell can do nothing more against a Church which only receives to give.

The adversary will therefore employ other means. After cupidity, he will use *Pride*. He uses it a lot. Pride scatters faith, pride undermines obedience ; by means of it the Church will indeed be destroyed !

Now, if one excepts St. Paul, the first preachers of the Gospel do not possess either diplomas or scientific degrees ; how will these ignorant men convince spirits, cultivated and refined by Greek philosophy ? Precisely because of their very ignorance, for thanks to it they will not be tempted to add anything to revealed doctrine. They will preach wholly and uniquely " what they have seen and what they have heard ". Their weakness became their strength.

How human is this Church, which in order to speak to men must borrow their language ! So human that her official language has for ages been a dead language ! Her weakness always becomes her strength :   the disadvantage in this matter also becomes an advantage, for her fixed language has always favoured the immutability of dogma.

Along with her dogmatic intransigence the Church manifests an equal intolerance to all that could damage her moral laws.   Rather than distort the precept of conjugal indissolubility for the benefit of Henry VIII, she prefered to see the whole kingdom of England pass into heresy.   One should always cite Pascal ;   " States would perish if laws did not give way to necessity now and then.   But religion has never suffered that or never made use of it . . there must be agreements or miracles. It is not strange that one should preserve oneself by giving way . . . . but that this religion always remained and was always inflexible, that is divine ".

Humanly uncertain of to-morrow, the Church has never been tempted to assure herself of her popularity with the crowds by a softening of the doctrine of Jesus Christ.   She would rather perish than agree to the slightest error :   And she has survived, without sacrificing a particle of her Credo.   She had to take a century to conquer Arianism, but she triumphed over it.   Pelagianism is near to putting out Pope Zosimus :   Pelagianism was conquered in its turn.   The Church eliminated one after another the heresies of the Middle Ages ;   she resisted the equally redoubtable influence of the pagan Renaissance and corroding Protestantism.   She kept intact her doctrinal patrimony in spite of the attacks or advances of the rationalism of the nineteenth century. Would a purely human society not have made some compromise with the ideas of the day ? While the thought of man has not ceased to evolve, how has the Church been able to maintain the integrity of her doctrine and that without being a stranger either to the Latin genius or Greek philosophy, or to that of the Middle Ages— capable on the contrary of making her doctrine intelligible to the spirits of every age, without ever modifying her teaching. Don't let us fool ourselves : heresies are not born outside the Church, but in her very bosom. It is her children who, more or less conscious victims of pride, reject the primitive teaching. It is her sons, the highest among them, who, victims of ambition, have brought about the schisms. The Church has seen them go away from her, with sorrow. She has lost whole countries successively, but what she loses in number, she soon gains in quality. Her least numerous sons are the most fervent and their fervour increases her numbers little by little. Instead of time altering her doctrine or enervating her disciples, the risk of disagreement diminishes with the centuries. Who would attempt to-day to start a new schism ? The authority of the Pope has never been as universally respected or as filially obeyed as in our day. The powers of Hell, it is true, have inflicted enormous losses on the Church, but they have not prevailed against her.

It remained for Hell to try to destroy the *holiness* of the Church, by debasing her morality. It is not difficult to make men sin ! The Church, in fact, has gone through periods of a saddening moral mediocrity. Meanwhile, even in those epochs, happily rare, when the highest dignitaries showed themselves unworthy of their sacred character, there were great numbers of saints in the Church and it is they who saved it. Whatever happened in the tenth, fifteenth or sixteenth centuries the Church always reformed herself, and the impartial observer must recognise that for the last four centuries Catholic holiness has become more general, and the Church does not grow only by spreading, but also in perfection.

*   *   *   *

Despairing of being able to corrupt Christian souls the powers of Hell have recourse to their supreme resource ; *persecution from without*. Our Lord made sure the Apostles were aware of this, " You will be persecuted, you will be dragged before tribunals, you will be beaten, you will be killed. Among every people, you will meet men who will hate you because of me : but have confidence, I have conquered the world ".

That prediction has also been fully realised. As soon as she was born in Jerusalem, the Church was persecuted by the Jews. For two and a half centuries the imperial might of Rome used every possible means of coercion against her : confiscation, exile, forced labour, capital punishment preceded by torture, of which Gaston Boissier could say, " after being astonished that there could be found judges to pronounce such frightful punishments against the Christians, one is no less surprised that the victims were able to bear them " [1] But far from slowing up the growth of the Church, the murderous persecution accelerated its rhythm. " We multiplied according as you decreased our numbers " ; wrote Tertullian, " the blood of the Christians is a seed " [2].

Now, persecution has been going on savagely against the Church all the time, in one country or another. The cruelties of the pagans of another day have been

---

[1] *La fin du paganisme,* vol. I, p. 370.
[2] *Apology,* 50.

surpassed by those of the communist executioners. Nevertheless *violence* never had the upper hand of the Church.

But the powers of Hell know how to change their tactics. One of their representatives proclaimed it lately in Parliament, " Free-masonry is eternal ! " Which means, " the forces of evil will never capitulate ". Our Lord had said it before him. The adverse powers make laws against the Church, some of which curb her action, others radically go against her. With more perversity still, they set themselves out to withdraw the souls and the hearts of the popular masses from Christian influence ; by a methodical seizure of the schools and the press.

Nothing will stop them in their campaigns of de-christianisation, neither the development of immorality, nor the appeal to the base passions of envy and hatred, whatever is the consequence of their campaigns. The destruction of families, social upheavals, war itself, will not dismay them if this is to be the price of the ruin of the Church. To crown their hypocrisy, the anti-christian sects will hide their intrigues behind a philo-sophic or pseudo-scientific façade.

In this struggle to the death, the Church fights valiantly, without counting her sacrifices, in order to protect her children against lies and error. Humanly she fights with unequal weapons, for money, favours, threats are not on her side. Humanly she ought to be conquered. Centuries ago the pontiffs of anti-christianity signed her death warrant.

In the time of St. Augustine the enemies of the Church were already declaring, " The Church is about to die, the Christians have had their day ". To which the bishop of Hippo replied, " Still it is they whom I see dying every day, while the Church remains continually upright, announcing the power of God to every succeeding generation ". " Another twenty years ", said Voltaire, " and the Catholic Church will be done for ". And twenty years later Voltaire died and the Church continued to live. " The Church ", wrote Jules Janin, " was quite sick before 1830, the Revolution of July killed it completely ! " Renan thought he would lay it out under flowers. *Orpheus* would certainly give it the final blow . . . So, since Celsus in the third Century, there has not been a generation in which the grave-diggers were not prepared to bury the Church, and the Church still lives. Montalembert said it magnificently in the Chambre des Pairs in 1845 : " Against all those who calumniate it, who enchain it or who betray it, the Catholic Church has a victory and an assured vengeance ; its vengeance is to pray for them and its victory is to survive them ".

Jesus did not cheat us. The gates of Hell will not prevail against His Church. Perpetually attacked, thwarted, harmed she continues her mission none the less, serenely and trustfully ; the mission that her divine founder entrusted to her. Her existence consists, according to the happy phrase of Fr. Faber " of a continual victorious defeat " [1]. Yes, she is human, our Church, so weak and always just on the brink of or just after a set-back ; but is she not divine, this Church, which regularly emerges victorious from all her defeats ? " There is a pleasure ", noted Pascal, " in being in a vessel, battered by the tempest when one is assured that it will never perish. The persecutions that torment the Church are of this kind ".

Brethren, let us never have doubts about our Church. Her history is a permanent miracle on which we can rest our faith. But if we believe that the Son of God lives in His Church, if we are persuaded that the Church

---

[1] *Bethléem*, vol. I, p. 105.

is the body of Christ, that the Church is Jesus and is us, don't let us be lulled into a feeling of security. Jesus asks us for the little help of our personal effort to contribute to the triumph of His Church over the powers of evil. It is up to us to reduce the infirmities that arise from our human faults, and to suppress the stains that hide the glory of her divinity from the world. To that end let us be, more and more, better sons of our Mother, the Church. Our pious ancestors in the Middle Ages never said baldly like us, " the Church " ; they said more prettily, " Holy Church ". It is to our holy Church that we owe the desires and the beginnings of holiness that, nonetheless, we recognise in each of us. Let each of us apply ourselves therefore, by a more loving manage-ableness, to making our dear Church always more holy !

CHAPTER IX

THE HUMAN HEAD OF THE DIVINE CHURCH.

And I will give to thee the keys of the kingdom of heaven ; and whatever thou shalt bind on earth shall be bound in heaven ; and whatever thou shalt loose on earth shall be loosed in heaven.

(Matt. XVI, 19.)

GOD wants to raise humanity up to Himself. His own Son, by joining the human race, united in a single human person the infinite divinity with our human nature. The Son of God became man, to make us, children of men, sons of God. The Incarnation will have an eternal morrow : the Church, through which we enter in our turn into the divine family.

The Church makes all the faithful members of a body of which Jesus Christ is the head. The Holy Ghost infuses divine life into it and binds each of us particularly to Jesus Christ. God alone, in fact, can be the author of our deification. The priest who baptises us is only an instrument of the divine action.

St. Paul, dealing with marriage, speaks to us of the love that Jesus Christ has for His Church ; " . . as Christ shewed love to the Church when He gave himself up on its behalf. He would hallow it, purify it by bathing it in the water to which His word gave life ; . . . in all its beauty, no stain, no wrinkle, no such disfigurement ; it was to be holy, it was to be spotless " [1]. For this work of sanctification, Christ created the priesthood in His Church, the transmittor of His own divine life.

---

[1] Eph., V, 25–27.

But sacerdotalism must have a governor ; there must be a visible power in the Church which co-ordinates and directs the activity of the apostles, which guards all the teaching of the Master in all its purity, which assures unity among all her members.

Jesus never wished this authority to be multiple, it was to rest on one man, Peter. Jesus will remain the unique Master of the kingdom which He has established on earth ; but Peter will be the sole manager, the major-domo to whom Jesus will entrust all the keys. The measures which he takes on earth will be ratified in Heaven, for His authority is the authority of Christ Himself. Jesus confers on Peter more than a primacy of honour over the other apostles : He invests him with an effective authority over the whole Church.

And what authority ! No one has ever been honoured with such a charge. Peter's power surpasses that of all the sovereigns. A monarch makes laws and levies taxes ; a despot can arrogate to himself the right of life and death over his subjects. The power of Peter is great in another way, for it is exercised over what escapes the most absolute or most tyrannical human authorities. Peter has power over spirits, over consciences, over souls. He reaches inside us. And he alone fixes the limits of this power without equivalent.

Peter will tell us whether we are faithful or not to the doctrine and the wishes of Christ, and our judgment must bow down before his. Peter is responsible for our faith, our sanctification, our eternity. He alone is judge of the decisions that his responsibilities force him to take.

Do not let it be supposed that this interpretation of the powers of Peter merely perpetuates a state of fact, resulting from the secular exercise of an authority which would be developed in the sense of an increasing central-isation and absolutism. The powers of the Roman Pontiff in our day are no more extended than those of Peter in the beginnings of the Church.

It is Peter who has a successor to the treacherous Apostle elected, Peter who speaks or who replies in the name of all. A Christian tries to cheat : hear in what terms he takes him up ; " How is it that Satan has taken possession of thy heart, bidding thee defraud the Holy Spirit . . ? " Peter insists ; " It is God not man, thou hast defrauded " [1]. And there and then Ananias, falls down and dies. To defraud Peter is to defraud God.

It is Peter, who in spite of the opposition of the first of the faithful in Jerusalem, decides to carry the Gospels to the pagans. Once more, at Antioch, Peter will hesitate. He will be afraid that his welcoming attitude to the pagan converts might trouble the faith of Christians come from Judaism. Paul will reproach him with this weakness, but without contesting the fact that Peter had the right to adopt successively two different solutions. Further, St. Paul, in order to win over those who doubt that he, the old adversary of the Church, can preach the Gospel to them, lets them know that he first went up to Jerusalem to know Cephas and that he stayed with him for fifteen days. And it is Peter—always—who presides over the first council held at Jerusalem in the year 51.

* * * *

Nineteen centuries have changed nothing, Brethren, of Our Lord's ruling. The destiny of the Church rests on a man, on one man.

To what risks did the Son of God not expose Himself ? This is how our short human prudence can reason. In

---

[1] Acts, V., 3–4.

reality, Jesus' imprudence was always wisdom. The last word of command from Jesus, you remember, is a moving call for unity ; " *Ut sint unum !* " But if He had many authorities at the head of His disciples, divergencies, even slight ones, could have arisen. This was an even more dangerous risk, to introduce coteries, parties, into the Church, and finally divisions. Christ remains the eternal head of the Church and the authority of Christ will never be divided because Jesus has delegated it to Peter alone. He chose a man, a single man, and as Peter has shown, a man subject to human weaknesses. When He is choosing him, Jesus knows that Peter will give in during the Passion. On the eve of the day when he denies Him, Jesus tells him that He has prayed for him so that his faith will never weaken, then he adds, " When, after a while, thou hast come back to me, it is for thee to be the support of thy brethren ".

The momentary weakness of Peter, foreseen by the Master, proves to us that in giving His Church a monarchical foundation, Jesus had weighed up all the risks. He knew that all the successors of Cephas would not be saints, that some would be the victims of ambition, of cupidity, or of less avowable passions still. However saddened we are by the indignity of a very small number of bad popes, it is a fact at least affirmed by historical documents, that not a single one of them was led away by the disorders of their private lives to relax the least precept of the moral law, not a single one among them tried to forgive their errors by letting the deposit of dogmatic truth be encroached upon.

Towards the end of the Fourteenth Century anarchy desolates the Church. Following a contested election anti-popes rise up against the popes. Christianity does not know whom to obey any more, the saints themselves have gone away : St. Catherine of Siena is for Rome, and St. Vincent Ferrier for Avignon. Popes and anti-popes call for power to the kings who are playing with them. A frightful epoch which justifies the cruel words of Lacordaire, " History is the long recital of the dishonours of men ". " A temporal kingdom ", wrote a Protestant author on this subject, " would, without doubt, have succumbed but the idea of the Papacy was so indestructible, that this split . . . only served to show its indivisibility." [1]

Should the faults of some make us forget the virtue, the science, the zeal of so many other pontiffs ? Around the statue which he is carving from precious wood, the sculptor lets lost fragments fall. We are not going to burrow in the debris, and reproach him for the useless waste instead of admiring the masterpiece which he has created.

A man, a single man, even if he is a saint, will never get rid of his personality. His opinions will always be influenced by his cast of spirit, his manner of governing will also depend on his temperament. This penalty of the unity of command did not escape Our Lord. It is true, that every Pope, however respectful of tradition, directs the Church in a certain spirit, that each reign has its ruling idea or ideas, and one can see, without any difficulty, difference of orientation from one pontificate to another. Differences, yes ; divergences, no, and contradictions, less still. The inconvenience that might arise from the too personal action of a single chief is admirably compensated by the succession of pontiffs who do not resemble one another. One will be bolder, another more timid ; this one will seem to be preoccupied with conquering the world for Christianity, that one will insist more on the interior formation of the faithful. But in this way, they complete each other marvellously as do the alternative movements of systola and diastola which regulate the circulation of the blood

---

Quoted by F. Mourret, *La Papauté*, p. 112.

in the whole system.

As to the fact of finding out whether, different as they are from one another, each is the authentic representative of the authority of Christ, history makes the reply that each pope comes at his hour, and that his genius accords providentially with the necessities of the moment.

The *Acts* teach us that the shadow of St. Peter cured the sick, gathered where he would pass, but his body would not have cast this shadow if God's sun were not shining behind him. Thus, the popes are only, but they are certainly, Christ's shadow : by whatever name he calls himself, Leo, Pius or Benedict—behind the head of the Church, we always see the light of God.

Brethren, the divine institution of the papacy is too certain a truth, for us to be able to neglect our duties as Catholics towards him whom we name the Holy Father. First of all there is *respect*. Because we know we will always see in him Christ whom he represents, we will not yield to the temptation, that is too easy, of opposing one pope to another, in order to place our trust only in those whose actions agree best with our personal tendencies. We will not be like those people, who regret yesterday's pope, or wait for to-morrow's, in order to excuse them from obeying to-day's head. Read the texts of the coronation of the pontiffs, you will notice that none confers the powers of his dignity on the man elected by the Conclave. The successor of St. Peter holds these powers directly from Christ. When we speak of the Sovereign Pontiff, let us banish terms borrowed from parliamentary assemblies, or the polemics of newspapers, from our vocabulary and not leave the duty of revealing to us the prestige that the head of Christianity exercises in the world to men who are strangers to our faith.

The respect with which we speak of the Pope will dispose us to *obeying him* more perfectly. There should, of course, be no question of discussing the truths over which his infallible magistery extends itself nor the orders emanating from his sovereign jurisdiction : one only belongs to the Church by submission. But like true sons, we will listen attentively to the simple counsels of the Father of the faithful and we will apply ourselves to putting them loyally into practice.

It may come about that one or other of the pontifical directions may interfere with our spiritual habits or claim the sacrifice of temporal interests that we believed were basic to us. In such a case, instead of pretending that we have a monoply of the truth, would it not be wiser if we first of all tried to understand our head's thought well ? The Pope sees higher and farther than us. This is why his word has an import that surpasses our particular views and such of his instructions as can astonish you respond in reality not only to the problems of to-day but also to the difficulties of to-morrow.

In any case, never let us lower ourselves to the extent of attributing to the head of the Church unfavourable intentions for any group of his sons, or favouritism directed to the advantage of another nation or those of another social class ; that would be to do him a grave injury.

Imagine for the moment the problems that pose themselves to the conscience of the Sovereign Pontiff. He knows that the least word he says will have gone around the world in a few hours : is he not going to weigh each of his words carefully—to avoid everything that might give rise to confusion—to soften, even if some (and there are always some) think the qualification excessive, to soften an expression which, incorrectly understood, might cause more harm than it would shed light ? It is not only his authority that he exercises in issuing an order or a defence, he knows that his will shall be executed by hundreds of thousands of the faithful whom one inopportune command could put astray.

Do you think that he can forget his responsibility? If he were only a man like one of us, he would only want to open his mouth after having consulted and interrogated, collected all opinions, and having personally studied and reflected. Which of us would dare to raise our voice in such conditions? Would we not prefer to remain silent? The Pope only speaks because he has a duty to do so, an imperative duty attached to his charge. Also he does not content himself with these long conferences with his conscience; he converses longer still with God, in a prayer in which his whole soul gives itself over, and only wants to give itself over, to the Holy Ghost. What is at stake for those who will not obey his word, is perhaps their eternal salvation. Who would suppose that he is going to speak lightly, or under the influence of human considerations? It is on his knees that he meditates the doctrine of his encyclicals. The condemnation that he must issue would never see the light of day if he had not the certainty that he must speak in the name of Christ.

I am convinced, Brethren, that there would be no more dissidents among the Catholics of our day if all would only try to reflect on this: the pope has a conscience, the conscience of an honest man, the conscience of a Christian, the conscience of a head (and what a head!) the representative of Christ before all Christians.

You need not look for any other proof that the Sovereign Pontiff is conscious of the responsibilities that are his, than the insistence with which he demands that we fulfil our third duty in respect to him, that of *praying with him and for him*. No Mass is celebrated without our mentioning his name. With a surprising generosity, he dispenses indulgences so that we may pray for his intentions. Do not let us see this as a superfluous recommendation, but let us assist him filially with our prayers.

Remember the touching scene of St. Peter in Chains. Some days before, Herod Agrippa had had Peter thrown into prison and was going to put him to death after the feast of the unleavened bread, when an angel caused the fetters to fall miraculously from the Apostle and brought him out of the prison. Freed, Peter reflected : he dared not go and look for James in Jerusalem, for they would certainly come and seize him again. So he went to the house of a humble woman, the mother of a man who was probably the Evangelist Mark. When he arrived there he found the house full of Christians who had been praying for him without stop, from the first day of his imprisonment.

Devotion to the Pope therefore dates from the very first days of the Church. Let us guard it carefully, it is the property of holy souls. Peter has need of two helps to direct the Church : the unfailing assistance of Christ and the humble prayer of all Christians.

CHAPTER X

THE APOSTLE OUGHT NOT JUDGE ACCORDING TO HUMAN STANDARDS.

At which He turned round and said to Peter? " *Back Satan, thou art a stone in my path ; for these thoughts of thine are man's, not God's.*"

(Matt. XVI, 23).

FIRMER now in our Catholic convictions, Brethren, we will know how to make better use of the riches of Christian dogma and our superhuman dignity as sons of God. Jesus' call from now on will resound more strongly within us : the call to sanctity, the call tô the apostolate. But the Christian, the apostle, must be like the Master, marked with the sign of the Cross. This is the general meaning of the teaching that Jesus is now going to give to Simon Peter, and to which we also need very much to listen.

The Gospel has just finished telling us Jesus' promises to His Apostle. It is on him that the Church will rest. The Saviour had given him absolute discretion, all Peter's decisions will be confirmed in Heaven. And merely four verses further on, the rock which the powers of Hell will not be able to shake, is no more than a stumbling block. Jesus thrusts the man, whom all will have to obey, out of His path, as if he were in league with the Adversary of God. " *Back Satan, thou art a stone in my path !* " What happened in the interval ?

The disciples know now that Jesus is the Son of God, but it was vital that Our Lord should warn them also of the true character of His mission. Knowing of His divine nature, were they not indeed going to expect more surely still the earthly triumphs inseparable ın their minds from the Messianic task ? The Master made haste to set them right on this point.

The deliverance that they were hoping for would not come about as they expected : the Messiah would only raise men up again by expiating their sins through His own sufferings. Up till now Jesus had only made veiled allusions to His redeeming death. "*From that time onwards*", writes St. Matthew, that is to say, immediately after the confession at Cesarea, "*Jesus began to make it known to his disciples that he must*" (He reveals the divine plan) "*go up to Jerusalem and there, with much ill-usage from the elders, the chief-priests and the scribes, must be put to death and rise again on the third day*".

The Apostles cannot believe their ears. Such an outlook does not accord either with the conception which they have of the Messiah, or, above all, with the revelation which they have just received about the personality of the Son of God. But perhaps they are more moved still by the idea of the sorrowful fate in store for their Master. Peter, who loves Him tenderly, is completely overwhelmed.

So Peter, "*drawing him to his side, began remonstrating with him . . . .*" This detail from the Gospel is exquisite. At the thought of the possible, close, death of Jesus, Peter forgets to keep his distance. The Greek text is no less touching, "Then *coming to comfort him*", Peter began to take him up on it . . ." He imagines that Jesus, feeling the hostility of which He is the object more strongly at that moment, has given way to a temporary fit of depression. "*Never, Lord, no such thing shall befall thee*".

Immediately the Master wrenches Himself loose from Peter's grasp. His language is as hard as the disciple's was affectionate ; He treats him as he did the tempter in the desert.

The situation is, in fact, identical : unwittingly Peter wants to turn the Saviour from His duty. A man like us, Jesus is naturally averse to the idea of dying ; naturally He can only be revolted by the idea of an unjust condemnation to death ; He will not be pretending in the Garden of Olives. But since He must go through with it, since it is the will of His Father, He cannot stand anyone, even when they are inspired like Peter by sentiments of the most faithful friendship, weakening His courage by trying to put the vision of His sacrifice away from Him.

Peter loved Him so much ! Friends are not always clairvoyant in their demonstrations of sympathy. Peter will prove it another time, when his affection for Jesus will lead him into the Praetor's courtyard, where he will deny Him. Sympathy is not necessarily a good counsellor. This is the case here. Peter, led astray by his good heart, has blundered ; his act is a trap into which Jesus does not want to fall. " Back, Satan ! thou art barring the route which the Father has mapped out for me, out of my way, thou art a stone in my path ! "

Poor Peter ! he did not know, he did not believe that he had done anything wrong ; besides, in the depths of his heart he continued to hope that nothing of all this would happen to his Master. This is why the latter keeps on reprimanding him. Just before when Simon confessed, " Thou art the Son of the living God ", he was not speaking like a man, he had been enlightened by the Father. This time, when he wants to strike another mystery, no less obscure, perhaps even more so than the Incarnation, the mystery of the Passion and the death of the Son of God, out of the providential plan, he is not listening to God, he is only obeying human impulses.

None of us, Brethren, would like to condemn Simon

Peter, and yet Jesus, who spoke to him so severely, knew all the goodness of the disciple better than we do. The apostle's crime was, as always, to follow his first impulse, to reason instinctively like a man, instead of setting himself first of all to understanding the divine teaching. We ought not lose sight of his mistake, nor the blame which it brought down on him.

In other circumstances, Jesus spoke of scandal in terrifying terms, because he envisaged then those who would intentionally pervert the candid souls of the little ones who believed in Him. Here, He teaches us that scandal does not consist only of disciples leading others to evil, but also when they turn others away from what is good, or might better them, by letting them be taken up by purely human preoccupations, and that also, without wanting to, without knowing it, neither giving advice, nor direct bad example, we can become an occasion of scandal for our brethren. This risk ought to give us reason for great circumspection.

The law of Moses forbade one to put a "scandal" or stumbling-block in the path of a blind man, that is to say a stone, or any trap which might make him stumble and fall.[1] The word is only used nowadays in a figurative sense, but it has kept its original meaning nevertheless : it is the occasion of a fall. Now there is scandal, not only when one leads another to evil-doing, either directly or indirectly, but also in all manner of speaking or acting which lessens the love, the practice, or the very notion of good in others. This was exactly Peter's fault. Now, this last aspect of scandal extends our responsibilities remarkably. It broadens them to the very extent of the Sermon on the Mount.

With his usual sense of proportion the Catholic theologian, without restricting our responsibilities, pro-

---

[1] *Leviticus*, XIX, 14.

tects us, at least, from excess of scruples. If others are scandalised wrongly by our actions, we cannot be held to blame for that. We ought to despise the pharisaical scandal completely : for example, if anyone makes our acts of piety or of zeal an excuse for blaspheming religion. At other times, our neighbour is scandalised, but that is because of his ignorance or through an error of judgement : in such a case, if one can do it without difficulty, it is better to stop giving scandal to the weak. " But not everything can be done without harm ", writes St. Paul, " I am free to do what I will, but some things disedify " [1]. But whoever has a valid reason for not modifying his manner of acting, however it astonishes others, ought to make as great an effort as possible to explain, to those, who were surprised by it, the proper basis of his conduct.

With these reservations, accorded to our legitimate liberty, we must be careful never to trouble the conscience of others, watching carefully that we do not lead them from good.

Whether we wish it or not, our acts have a posterity which concerns us. Everything we say is a profession of faith ; everything we do is a pleading, an encouragement, an allurement in favour of good, or of less good, or of evil. We influence, first of all, our immediate circle, then, many of our intimates. The stone thrown into the pond does not merely disturb the water in the spot where it hits it. Around the point of impact one can see great concentric circles forming, and widening till they reach the bank. In the same way, all our words and all our action have far-off repercussions that we never even suspect. Perhaps a great reward is waiting for us in heaven, for having one day, without noticing it, given a good example. But neither can we measure

[1] 1 Cor., X, 23.

the evil influence of a word that escaped us, or an
unthinking gesture which was not what it ought to have
been, both of them quickly regretted, and not even
remembered.

Our responsibilities increase, besides, according to the
privileges we receive from God and from men. If the
reflexion that brought the harsh reproval of Jesus down
on the future head of the Church, had come not from
him, but from one, say, of the holy women, the Master
might not even have taken her up on it. On Peter's
lips he judged it to be inadmissible. Thus, the gravity
of our responsibilities depends on our situation, the
prestige we enjoy, the respect granted to us, the rights
that authority or friendship confer on us. This is why
we should never lose sight of the influence we exercise
over others, which can easily become for them a cause
of scandal, instead of contributing to their edification.
And, once more, we are not talking here about evil,
positively suggested, but of good, indirectly hindered.

Simon Peter, through the goodness of his soul, wanted
to prevent Jesus from suffering. In doing so, he hid
His duty from Him. Let us also watch out that we do
not lessen the *notion of good* in others, even when we are
only striving after what we believe to be their interests.

For example, to reassure someone one will be tempted
to lessen the failings of which he is accusing himself,
" You acted in good faith . . . . God forgives you for
your intentions ". But, by taking away from a guilty
person the motives which brought about his repentance,
at the same time one robs him of the stimulus that would
be most active in raising him up again. Or else in order
to encourage someone, you exaggerate the quality of
his work, and hide imperfections from him that he could
easily avoid without bother ; you assure him that he
has done his duty quite well, much more than many

others and that God is not as demanding as he thinks. What Christian is there who has not reproached himself for doing too much for religion and God has not asked him to do as much again ? For these pretended encouragements have as their result a diminishing of our courage, a lessening of our ideal, and they make us slide towards mediocrity.

Duty has limits fixed by God ; it is not for us to restrict them even in a mood of charity. The affection that we bear our brethren demands that we believe them to be capable of fulfilling all their duties and that we help them by showing them that they can really do so, by teaching them how to perform them better. We cannot know what God expects from a man : it is not, therefore, for us to determine the perfection to which he ought to strive. On the contrary, by always putting duty at a high level, we will permit our brothers to become greater.

The scandal of which we are speaking does not only attack the notion of duty, but also *the practice of good*.

We all have our heights and our depths, our hours of high spirits and our days of depression. Now it is not infrequent that, in the moments when we have no energy or spirit, we are led to confide the tale of all our failures and our deceptions to those who came to us, perhaps, for consolation. We plunge them into a bath of bitterness. They hoped to revive their faith and they found us uncertain, if not sceptical. They had counted on us communicating a little of our zeal to them, and here they heard us sighing and coming out with the " what's the use " of the disillusioned.

I do not say that in such circumstances it would be better to be silent . . . that would be too little. I say that if one of our brothers comes to us looking for help in his weakness, at a moment when we are completely in pieces ourselves, God sends him to us to make us blush at our weakness and to rouse us out of it as soon as possible. However stricken we are by our own task we ought not present a man, who is hesitating before a difficult duty, with the spectacle of our own confusion. Let us recover ourselves quickly, and he will rally at the same time as we do. Let us give ourselves over only to what will do good to others, and this will make us immediately more believing, more courageous, more generous. Do not let us ever show off our miseries under the pretext of humility. One of the ways of making reparation for our faults is not to talk of them to others, but to use our unhappy experiences in order to avoid falling again.

Scandal, finally, is everything that would tarnish *the love of good* in others. " Do not stifle . . . the Spirit ", recommends St. Paul[1]. Do not let us blow on the flames that burn in the heart of man ! There are stiflers of enthusiasm that motives of envy or interest lead to that sad occupation. Such people cannot be Christians. But others believe that they are speaking in the name of prudence, who destroy generous initiative by prophesying the inconveniences, the disappointments, the reverses that will attend its author. " You are young ", these envious spirits say, " you will find out . . . " Others, through lightness of spirit, give way to the pleasure of being ironic at the expense of the " visionaries " who hope to reform the world, or the " madmen " who busy themselves bringing help to their fellow-men.

Never let us kill hope in the heart of men. Never let us smother the idealism of the convinced. Never let us stifle the beautiful ardours of charity. Let us respect the faith of the apostles and the thirst for holiness of

---

[1] 1 Thess., V, 19.

those whom the madness of the cross sweeps away. They are above us, and I do not know what sentiment, which is at the heart of all the sons of Adam, could bring us perhaps to look for the weak point, the irregularity in those who surpass us. But if we know how to rejoice because there are men better than us, if we are sincerely happy to see them more faithful to God than us and more like Christ, those who surpass us will soon draw us after them.

Let us pray often, Brethren, for those whom we have scandalised, perhaps, sometimes by wilfully inducing them to evil, but more often without doubt, by leading them astray wittingly or inadvertently. Let us ask our Lord to correct our too natural outlook, our too human considerations, so as not to let us be guilty of barring for others, or mistaking ourselves, the path by which He wants to bring men to holiness.

CHAPTER XI

IN THE SHADOWS AS IN THE LIGHT.

Peter said to Jesus? " *Master, it is well that we should be here ; let us make three arbours in this place, one for thee, and one for Moses and one for Elias* ". *But he spoke at random.*

(Mark IX, 4–5 ; Luke IX, 33).

As the first part of Jesus' ministry had been inaugurated by the voice from on high which, on the day of His baptism, pointed Him out as the Messiah : " *Thou art my beloved son* ", the second period, which ends with His sorrowful redemption, also opens with a divine manifestation. Once more God is heard to say, " *This is my beloved Son, to him, then, listen !* " Believe in Him, He is truly My Son. Hear when He announces the deliverance through His sufferings. This second theophany was more discreet and at the same time more solemn.

Jesus only admitted three Apostles to it : Peter, James and John, the same who will be the witnesses of His anguished prostration at Gethsemane. Meanwhile he gathered together the two great heroes of Israel, Moses and Elias, who represented the Law and the Prophets, and all three *spoke of the death which he was to achieve at Jerusalem*. The Apostles could learn therefore that Jesus would not be the victim of a sudden attack by His enemies. His sacrifice was quite foreseen, willed by Heaven, in full accord with those who in the Old Testament spoke under God's orders.

It was necessary that the approaching humiliations

of the Saviour and His apparent failure should not make the disciples doubt His divinity. This is why Jesus wants to let them foresee a ray of His glory. " *His face shining like the sun, and his garments becoming white as snow* ", says Matthew, " *white as no fuller here on earth* ", writes Mark, " *could have made them* ".

This miracle, which came a few days after Peter's confession at Cesarea, must never have gone out of his mind : thirty-five years later he will evoke, for the recipients of the second Epistle, what he witnessed " when he was with Jesus on the holy mountain " [1].

But the Gospel lets us know the reflection that escaped the spontaneous Apostle once again. He had not completely renounced his dream of a glorious Messiah. Here was the eagerly expected glory ! " Oh, Master, *it is well that we should be here !* We will build three huts with branches." And Peter already sees the crowds wending their way up the mountain-side to these improvised tabernacles to adore the Son of the living God who manifested Himself to His people . . . . Peter had not understood, and doubtless, confessed it ingenuously when he recalled this miracle, for St. Mark and St. Luke did not invent this detail ; they were reporting the Apostle's preaching when they recorded his contempt in their narrative : " *Peter spoke at random* ".

What he said, Brethren, which of us would not have thought it in his place ? For months Peter had to submit to the discussions of Jesus' adversaries, hearing their criticism and their perpetually renewed demands : and, now finally, he receives the visible proof of his Master's divinity. Oh, how good it is to know certitude, at last ! . . His Master who was attacked, decried, villified, has just let the veils that hid His splendour fall lightly to the earth. This is not yet the final revelation, face

---

[1] II Peter, I, 18.

to face, but at least a flight towards heaven. Should
Peter not want this vision to be prolonged ? Master,
how lovely it is ! Let us taste the exalted joys of this
fellowship for some time ! After the long fatigues of
the journey, grant us the rest of contemplation ! . . . .

But Peter was talking at random. Jesus was about
to break His disciple's enchantment immediately. A
cloud covered the three dismayed disciples, who fell
face forward on the ground. The voice of the Father
resounds. And when they lift their heads, they only
see Jesus alone, their every-day Jesus.

Peter was talking at random. It would certainly have
been " pleasant " for him, and comforting, to remain
in ecstasy, but this would not have been " good " for
him. What was good for Peter was the return to work
which awaited Jesus at the foot of the hill, the instruction
of an ignorant people, the healing of the sick, the hope
to be brought to the unfortunate. The work of the
Saviour was not to end in the glory of Thabor, but on
dark Golgotha, not among Moses and Elias, but between
two thieves.

What was good for Peter was to assist at the cruel
Passion of his Master, the humble repentance that
followed his denial of Him ; and the shadows of Calvary ;
and the anxiety of the three days that Jesus spent in the
tomb ; and the crushing brightness of the Resurrection.
It was, after the outpouring of the Holy Ghost, a whole
life of preaching and persecutions, his apostolate and
his martyrdom. The transfiguration of the Saviour
was to help him to accomplish all the sacrifices, not to
exempt him from a single one.

Jesus did not grant the inconsidered request of Simon
Peter for " Heaven is not on this side of the tomb " [1].
Peter wanted *vision* but, down here, our condition is to

[1] R.P. Faber, *Oeuvres posthumes*, Vol. II, p. 333.

believe without seeing. Peter wanted *beatitude* without shadow, but, on our earth, joys are mingled with sorrows and we go to happiness through *suffering*. Peter wished for *rest*, but we will have eternity to rest ourselves : the law of this life is *labour*. Jesus does not accept the protection of branches that Peter proposes to Him. Peter has first to build " His Church ".

The passing error of the Apostle ought not make us fall into a false contempt. We would not be the beings that God destines to partake of His glory if we did not feel an avid need for light, happiness and peace. The illusion is not to aspire to this, but to suppose that we can possess it immediately, in the infinite degree in which we want it.

On this earth, we are like travellers, journeying through the night. We just see enough to recognise our route. Sometimes the sky is covered over to such an extent that we cannot even distinguish this any more and our progress slows up or we go astray. Then, from time to time, lightening separates the clouds : by its flash we find the road again from which we were about to stray or which we had just left. But its light was as quick and short as it was bright and we must continue in the dark.

Such is the effect of the supernatural consolations of which God does not deprive any of his children, unforgettable graces, which suddenly brighten our consciences, bring new warmth to our hearts, transfigure our souls, intermittent graces however, and always of short duration. Heaven is not on this side of the tomb.

I.—Tormented by the enigmas that present themselves in the human soul, we should like a decisive response to all our queries. In reality, we need to " see ". The genius of man, with an admirable tenacity, discovers one after another the mysteries of nature and the secrets

of the history of our planet. But however extended his
field of knowledge may be, he is necessarily bound by
the limits of the facts subject to his control. The realities
which surpass these limits cannot be seized by the same
means of investigation : there is then no other natural
guide than reason, and the latter, which tries to explore
the infinite, is incapable of penetrating and grasping
it. To see and understand God, that is Heaven. God
reveals enough of Himself to us for us to adore Him and
to direct ourselves to Him by fulfilling the task which
He assigns to us in His Creation. His revelations give
us a good enough idea of the work which He has entrusted
to us. In spite of everything, we suffer, like St. Paul :
" since we recognise that our spirits are exiled from the
Lord's presence so long as they are at home in the body,
with faith, instead of a clear view, to guide our steps " [1].

From time to time God approaches us more directly
and there are no true believers who have not had
experience of this. In the course of a more composed
meditation, or a more trusting prayer, or without our
expecting it and through a pure effect of His mercy,
God, in some way, lets us touch Him. We have had an
unequivocal certainty of His presence in the world or
within ourselves. It was not the result of an overheated
imagination for, in general, He only appears to us like
this at moments when we are particularly lucid, and often
to order what we should hate with all our being to do.
It was indeed He. We have felt God . . . . Like Peter,
we should have liked this impression to have lasted
for ever. But the mists closed in again, immediately.
Then we are afraid that we were the victim of an illusion
or we claim that God has withdrawn His support from
us. We ought, on the contrary, to thank Him for having
sent us this illumination for an instant, and thence-
forward to follow the sole indications of the faith with

---
[1] II Cor., V, 6–7.

a strengthened docility . . . Heaven is not on this side of the tomb.

II.—On this side of the tomb, we ought to accept our share, greater or smaller, of more or less bitter sufferings. Let us not grumble against what we might take as indifference on the part of Him Who wished to be called our Father. It is always His voice which says in our conscience : Be righteous. It is He also who fashioned the heart of man that it might be happy. There was no discord intended between these two divine wishes. The promise of happiness is as certain as the obligation to be good is imperative. Both are narrowly bound together : man ought to find his joy in doing good. In this union of felicity and virtue, which is God's order, man regains his balance and the perfect achievement of his nature.

But down here, man is an unfulfilled creature. Throughout his life he must work himself for his own completion. The disorder of sin has put the normal link between goodness and happiness awry, and man must bring about the sorrowful reparation. Meanwhile let us be fair : God never leaves us without joy, for deprived of all joy, we would not be able to live ; but the joys that gladden our short lives are only ephemeral lights, the transfigurations of an instant that gleam on the road leading to Happiness. We would like our joys to last for ever. Lord, how good it is to be here ! We are talking at random. Joy that does not end belongs to a sphere, to which we have not yet entered. We are purchasing it at this moment by our faithfulness to the divine commands. We are not in Heaven yet ; let us take with Peter, the road that Our Lord Himself followed. It is not from Thabor, but from Calvary that He went up to His glory.

III.—For us, as for Peter, it is good to work and to struggle in order to gain a victory and a rest of which the present life can only give us a foretaste.

Certainly, it would give us great pleasure to be able, at this moment, to triumph over everything that trammels or compromises our union with God, and to arrive at a solidly established virtue. But in this life we have to earn that triumph. Dangers surround us on every side and we are never sure of ourselves : the awakening of a passion or some unexpected occasion can put our deep-seated weakness on trial. And yet, what graces we receive ! The Church showers them on us with such generosity ! Others might doubt their efficacy : the believers, at least, know the strength that they have communicated to them. You could all cite, Brethren, instances in your lives when God, having overwhelmed your hearts completely, made you capable of a duty which had dismayed you.

The truth is that the graces are the transfigurations destined to give us the strength to co-operate afterwards, with all our power, with the will of God. The Eucharist is the pledge of Heaven. Not yet Heaven possessed, but the sovereign help which will assist us in conquering it with a high hand. The sacrament of Penance helps us not to sin any more, but without making us sinless. It is up to us to watch out, to deaden our passions, to renew the necessary renunciations. God comes to our aid as soon as we pray to Him, but His help does not authorise us to be idle ; on the contrary, it incites us to more obstinate and more methodical efforts.

Let us accept the conditions of life that God has made ; Jesus Himself conformed to them. With Him, let us fulfil our destiny laboriously in humility, in patience, in work ; in other words, in sacrifice. Peter did not know what he was saying when he asked " to stay here ". We are fooling ourselves in the same way, by wanting to possess immediately what God promised at the end of our period of trial. And what is the important thing, here or there, on Thabor or on Calvary, in light or in sorrow ? What matters, what is good, is not to be here or there, it is always to be with Jesus.

CHAPTER XII

CHARITY HAS NO LIMITS.

Then Peter came to Him and asked " Lord, how often must I see my brother do me wrong, and still forgive him ; as much as seven times ? Jesus said to him, I tell thee to forgive not seven wrongs, but seventy times seven ".

(Matt. XVIII, 21–22.)

WHAT would we not give, Brethren, for the Saviour's acquaintances to have given us some memories of those intimate conversations during which Jesus undertook the individual education of His Apostles ! Without doubt, He tells them to preach from the roof-tops what He is teaching them in private ; but we would have loved to have taken part in the cross-fire of questions and answers, in the astonished interruptions of His listeners, and the Master's patient explanations. Here and there, the Gospel lets us know the questions that the Apostles posed to Jesus to try and understand His doctrine better. It is one of these that Simon Peter addresses to Him one day on the subject of the mutual forgiveness of offences.

This subject is one of these which are closest to the heart of the Master. It occupies an important place in the Sermon on the Mount and Our Lord puts the duty of forgiveness into the very text of the prayer which He taught us. But the instinct for revenge is so rooted in the animal part of our being that human pride makes it a point of honour to satisfy its grudges and considers it cowardice not to reply to outrage with outrage. So Jesus had to come back more than once to this article in his doctrine that is in such flagrant opposition to our natural reactions.

Simon Peter's inquiry is not so conspicuous if one does not separate it from the context in which the Evangelist puts it. According to St. Matthew, after having recounted the parable of the Lost Sheep, in which He shows God's joy when He can pardon a single sinner, Jesus specifies the attitude of the disciples when an offence is committed against them. He notes particularly the case of the brother, who, remaining stubborn in his ill-will, compromises his right to forgiveness. Conciliatory measures, appeals to the Church, have not brought about a reconciliation ; let him be considered like the heathen or the publican, " *what the Apostles have bound on earth, will be bound also in heaven* ". To all that Peter makes no objection.

But Jesus also said : " If thy brother does thee wrong, go at once and tax him with it as a private matter between thee and him ; and so, if he will listen to thee, thou hast won thy brother ". An admirable precept and how attractive ! But is it universally obligatory, and if so would it not give rise to abuses ? On the other hand, Our Lord lays such insistence on charity that Peter judges it necessary to enlarge on the Jewish tradition which obliged one to forgive a guilty person three times : " *Lord* ", he asked him, " *how often must I see my brother do me wrong and still forgive him ; as much as seven times ?* "

Jesus does not raise His voice, one can even imagine that a smile must have accompanied His reply, " *Not seven times, but seventy times seven* " Peter understood the light ironic point. Of course, it is not a question of counting to four hundred and ninety. One must always forgive. But Jesus guards His words, " This is why ", He adds (it is because one must forgive indefinitely) that in the kingdom of heaven, it will be like " a king who resolved to enter into a reckoning with his servants . . . "

Then He told them the story of the insolvent debtor, who moved his master to pity and had his debt remitted. This man, then, meeting one of his companions, who owed him a tiny sum, seized him by the throat, would accept no delay in payment and had him thrown into prison. Learning of this, the Master sent for the merciless servant once more : " I remitted all that debt of thine, thou wicked servant, at thy entreaty ; was it not thy duty to have mercy on thy fellow-servant, as I had mercy on thee ? " Angrily, the king hands him over to the torturers until he has paid all.

" *It is thus that My heavenly Father will deal with you, if brother does not forgive brother with all his heart*".

The moral of this parable is completed with the reply to Peter's question. " *How many times must I forgive ?* " —" *With all thy heart* ", replies the Saviour, who clears up and resolves the question by changing it, in order to make His disciples see it in the same light as He does. Let us apply ourselves, Brethren, to penetrating the Saviour's thought. It not only regulates the forgiveness of offences, which is what we are concerned with here, it also settles for us the very notion of good and the extent our charity should have.

It is worthwhile noting beforehand that Jesus is not dealing here with the conditions on which a guilty person has a right to forgiveness. It goes without saying that such a person cannot count on the mercy of his brother unless he recognises his guilt, repents and is sincerely disposed to make reparation. One could, without falsifying the Evangelic law at all, imagine the case of a delinquent, who would never once deserve forgiveness. This is how Peter will later judge Ananias and Saphira.

The present lesson is not concerned with the offender but only with the offended. Wronged, I have already been indulgent so many times to my repentant brother. Yet when he still persists in his misdeeds how often ought I to forgive him? Seven times? The measure proposed by Simon Peter may appear rather excessive to many, especially when it is a question of serious offences and particularly among strangers. In contrast, the ordinary bonds of society, family life, above all, afford, perhaps milder, but much more frequent occasions for grievances. Jesus takes no heed of these distinctions. His precept is absolute, it is valid for all situations.

Peter suggests a limit, and it is, precisely, the idea of a limit that Jesus will not admit. To forgive up to a certain point is not to forgive with all one's heart, and even less, is it to forgive as God forgives us.

Let us suppose, in fact, that Peter's proposition is made into a rule ; we will forgive our neighbour seven times only. Would it be foolish to suggest that some people might even be in a bit of a hurry to count to seven? I mean, may they not exaggerate the other's failings? May they not see malice in some previous questionable affair in order to make a real offence out of it? Is it unheard-of for people to interpret the silence of another as intended to be deliberately hurtful? As long as we rely on self-love, we will quickly arrive at number seven. And even if one avoided cheating, in order to count conscientiously up to seven, then, at a child's eighth impertinence, at the eighth row between husband and wife, or simply when one of our acquaintances has been lacking in respect to us seven times, we immediately discover that we have a right to give in to our old instinct for revenge? We are authorised to humiliate the guilty party, to withdraw not only our confidence from him, but also our affection. We can, without a scruple, cast him out of our lives and ignore him for ever. We can even, under pretext of punishment, render him evil for evil, make little of him, harm him. And all this, saying that we are Christians.

You notice that the two things are mutually exclusive, that one cannot believe oneself to be a disciple of Christ and at the same time suddenly have the right not to love a single one of one's brethren. It is this pretended right, this monstrous contradiction, that Jesus wanted to do away with in refusing to let us put a limit to the duty of forgiveness. A Christian has no choice : he is compelled to substitute fraternal love for self-love, for he must only judge and act with the spirit and the sentiments of Jesus Christ.

This is why our Lord does not think that he is giving us a model which it will be impossible to imitate, when He orders us to base our indulgence towards our brothers on the mercy with which God grants forgiveness to us. Compared to the offence that sin gives to God, the injustices of which men are guilty towards each other are only the little debt of a hundred pieces of silver of which the parable speaks. In relation to God, on the contrary, we are only insolvent debtors. An injury, an act of negligence of which God is the object, because they have offended His infinite holiness, are themselves irreparable.

Meanwhile God forgives us. On our repentance He tears up the account ; we do not owe Him anything any more ; He has forgotten everything. How often have we had to retract our indifferences, our disobedience, our forgetfulness, fully given in to ? Seven times or seventy-seven times seven ? In every case God forgives with the same generosity, without restriction, without reserve, without taking note of the promises we had made Him, and which we had not kept, without raising the least doubt as to the future of our new resolutions, " *I remitted all that debt of thine at thy entreaty* ". It is enough that we pray to Him to forgive us.

His forgiveness is the sign of His love, and love, whether it is human or divine, does not calculate. By forgiving us, God means all the time, to make us participate in His immense Goodness. He purifies our hearts in order to transform them. His Grace wishes to help us to destroy the empire of sin in us. And if His love for us cannot make us sinless, He, at least, expects our love for Him to make us patient and charitable towards the weaknesses of men, sinners like ourselves. If we cannot give Him a love equal to the one He bears us, He, at least, asks us to accord to our brethren a kindness, which like His own, has no calculation about it. Let us love them, let us forgive them from the bottom of our hearts.

Sinners on whom the divine mercy is exercised without stop, sinners whom the divine grace has made into other Christs, Christians, there are no two ways for us to treat those of our brethren who are sorry for having wounded or injured us ; we must forgive them always and with all our hearts.

But to do or to give something with all one's heart does not merely mean that there is no holding back, when one puts one's heart in a job, one does it with animation and gaiety.

The Christian ought therefore to forgive not only always and fully but, like God, joyously. We ought to be happy to wipe out our neighbour's wrongs, to do away with old scars, happy to spread the reign of peace and charity on earth, happy with the same joy that ravishes heaven every time that, on our little earth, a single sinner repents.

By way of conclusion, Brethren, we can notice that in forbidding us to limit the law of the forgiveness of offences, Our Lord gives us an instruction which is valid for all the commandments of the Gospel. " To forgive as we are forgiven ", is the application of the general principle : " To love as we are loved ".

Peter was mistaken in believing that he could limit the obligation to forgive. The characteristic of Christ's moral, its originality, its difficulty also—in short, His divine authority—all consist in the fact that in the accomplishment of good, there are no limits. Duty does not make demands on us only to a certain point, we will not be virtuous to a certain degree, no more than one can be honest to a limited extent. To set out to follow Christ without the intention of never leaving Him, would be to risk leaving him very soon. Good, as Jesus has let us know it and as He wants us to practice it, does not admit of limits : " Love as you are loved, without measure ".

This affirmation is not contradicted in anything by the rules of moral theology, which can foresee exceptions to a law or which distinguishes whether the breach of a precept constitutes a mortal or a venial sin. There you are then, it will be objected : standards, therefore limits.

Assuredly, but please observe on which side the limits have been drawn. Not on the side of obedience, but of disobedience, not on the way of good, but on the road of sin. The theologians say : at such and such a degree you fail grievously in your duty : mortal sin. At this other degree, you have not satisfied your obligations entirely but this insufficiency does not go beyond the limit of venial fault. At this third degree finally, you have obeyed the precept.

The Church must, in fact, enlighten consciences, and prevent them at the same time from restricting the obligations of the moral law and from exaggerating them. Far from falling under the reproach that Our Lord made to the Pharisees, loading men's shoulders with burdens that they would not touch themselves with their finger-tips, the Church, whose mission is to make mankind holy, knows that perfection is not the work of one day, and although she is anxious for sanctity for all her children without exception, she does not make a universal law out of it. She does not confuse the end with the point of departure. Her moral prescriptions mark out the points of departure, on this side of which one would infringe the law. The Church fixes the limits *beyond which* you must go, not those *as far as which* you can go. The sole limits she imposes are those that prevent us from falling into sin. When she tells us : " You have fulfilled the precept ", our conscience need not be disquieted any longer, but our heart still ought to be uneasy.

For, after that, the Church hands us over directly to grace. If we ask her to what point we can advance on the way of good, she replies to us like the Saviour that it is for our heart alone to decide. Outside strict duty, love makes up new duties, always surpassing themselves, for love does not calculate. Virtue begins with the exact observation of the law, but it only blooms outside the precept, in the freedom of discovering the desires and intentions of good, in the joy of refusing nothing to the holy will.

To what extent should I forgive ? How much should I put up with ? To what point should I give myself up ? These questions have no sense for the Christian who wants to love God as God has loved him. It is a big enough sign of our imperfections to set limits to the good *that we do ;* the true disciple of Christ does not set any to the good *that he wants to do.* He wants it always, totally and with all his heart.

CHAPTER XIII

THE APOSTLE'S REWARD.

Hereupon Peter took occasion to say, And what of us who have forsaken all, and followed Thee ; what is left for us ?
(Matt. XIX; 27–29). Similar passages
Mark X, 28–31 ; Luke XVIII, 28–30.

THIS new question of Simon Peter's to Jesus ought not make us suspect interested motives in the apostle, less still a vague sentiment of regret, a furtive look backwards. The context of the Gospel narrative acquits him of any such second thoughts. Peter is not looking backwards, he is looking forwards : *what will become of us ?*

The Gospel has just told the story of the conversation between Jesus and the rich young man who wanted to possess eternal life : keeping the commandments was not enough for him, he wanted to be perfect. The Saviour shows him the means ; that he should give his riches to the poor and come and follow Him. At these words, the young man goes away in sorrow because he has great possessions.

Jesus cannot keep from warning the disciples of the obstacle that the love of riches will raise before the Gospel. "Children", He tells them, "it is not easy to enter into the Kingdom of God. It is easier for a camel to pass through a needle's eye than for a rich man to enter in the Kingdom of Heaven when he is rich ". The disciples are stupified, they wonder among themselves. " On these conditions then, who can be saved ?" Jesus fastens his eyes on them and replies to their alarm : " Such a thing is impossible to man's powers, but to

God all things are possible ".

This is where Peter intervenes. " And what of us ?
What will become of us, who were not so rich, but who
renounced the little we had in order to follow you ?
We, who did not hesitate, as that rich young man did,
to abandon all, shall we enter into the Kingdom of
God ? If men, on their own, are incapable of saving
themselves, shall we belong to those whom God will
save, we who left everything when you said to us
" Come, follow me ? "

One cannot discover any thoughts of doubt in Peter's
query. He really has no doubt either about the Saviour's
previous promises or, in consequence, about the usefulness of the sacrifice that he and his companions have
made. He does not doubt, but he has, none the less,
a need to be reassured. The frankness of his character
makes him say out what he feels in his heart. In spite
of everything, he cannot but feel a little uneasiness :
" *And what of us ?* "

Notice, too, that at this moment Jesus and His Apostles
are a short distance from Jerusalem. The hour is
approaching when Jesus ought to begin the messianic
kingdom. Now the Master twice already—and He
will shortly do it a third time—has declared that his
triumph will not take place until after His death : "*He
will rise again on the third day* ". Before that, He will
be seized, buffetted, scourged and condemned to the
torture of the cross. This was not what the Apostles
hoped for when they left their boats on Lake Tiberias
and took leave of their families. They had only left
everything because they counted fully on being associated
in the Messiah's triumph. In these new conditions,
" *what is left for us ?* "

Peter does not complain. He knows now what he
did not know all along, that Jesus is the Son of God ;
nevertheless, their own future seems terribly uncertain

to him. If Jesus, the Son of God, must be crucified—
although they cannot yet fully grasp this idea—what
fate is in store for those who followed Him faithfully
from the first day ? . . . .

Isn't Simon Peter, Brethren, truly one of us ? Aren't
we grateful to him for having said out loud what we
sometimes think very quietly. And the Gospel would
not have reported his interruption if it were not to
reassure us in our turn.

*   *   *   *

Obviously, we cannot boast like the Twelve that we
have left all to follow Jesus. Yet it is no less true that
one cannot be His disciple at least without having given
up something for Him. Renunciation is the only way
into lived Christianity, which is true Christianity.

Now it is not the moment that one resolves on a
sacrifice that is the most costly. It dismays more and
more the longer one puts off its accomplishment. From
the moment one consents to it, divine grace makes one
aware above all of the alleviation, the liberation, that
are its fruit. The love of God, of which it is the sign,
dominates all the other sentiments of our hearts to such
an extent that in a way it deadens the pain caused by
sacrifice. But the wound is reopened later, most often
under the form of sharp and passing attacks, which are
only temptations from which one escapes quickly,
renewing one's offering. Sometimes, however, the
impression of bitterness which follows the sacrifice
betrays a real diminution of fervour, resulting itself
from imprudent glances backwards ; regrets, desires,
which are already a taking-back of what one had
generously offered to God. To tell the truth, it is
regretting a sacrifice that makes one feel the grief of it.
The Christian, who is absolutely faithful to the severity

of the rule of morals can certify, without a shadow of falsity, that the Lord's yoke is mild and his burden light. It is enough, alas, to break in on its intransigent rigour so little, for the law, until then mild, to become a weighty chain. And from the moment that one drags it regretfully, one cannot shake it off.

Individual chastity is not, besides, the sole obligation of Christian morality. The latter imposes numerous laws on us which are more or less sacrifices that one can indeed promise once and for all, but that one cannot do once and for all. One's promise must be kept day after day, and the hour comes for many when they hear inside themselves the voice of instinct that is starting to get the upper hand once more. Why all these sacrifices? Does God really demand them? Must one give up so many immediate joys for a future happiness?

"You want them too pure, the blessed you are making, and when their joy comes, they have suffered too much . . . . "

You race after these vague ideas, obsession with which leads infallibly to the loss, at least momentarily, of faith. However, have not good Christians discovered that by following Jesus Christ they have been brought further than they thought they would? When they attached themselves to Him, they were not aware that such hard sacrifices would be demanded of them one day.

The sacrifice is hard for the married couple, when, at the time of trial they recognise the flaw in the gold of their alliance : it will never ring true. Ah ! if it could be done again ! But that is exactly what cannot be done, it cannot be remade, the sworn faith must be kept.

Don't you also know young girls who had decided only to marry a sincerely Christian man ? For that they have refused reputedly advantageous matches, and then, no one presents himself and the years pass ! They had not supposed that their resolution would bring them so far ! Ought I not have been less strict ? they think. If it were to be done again ! . . . . . .

If you had another chance, Christians, would you still obey the noble scruples which made you despise those crooked ways of enriching yourselves ? Your rivals, your friends, did not have your refinement ; to-day they are well set-up while you, because of your probity, find it hard enough to feed your family. Certainly, you do not regret having been honest but there are days when one cannot help oneself thinking it a bit hard that the honest people should all seem to have been fooled.

Regret for past sacrifices because of the prejudice or the suffering they have brought on us, is never acknowledged without a certain shame which already condemns the complainer. There are other circumstances when our complaint, more similar still to Peter's, is based on the thought that our sacrifices, joyously-accepted, never withdrawn, have, however, never produced the good we expected from them for others and even for the cause of Jesus Christ.

It has been thought that it is enough to give oneself with all one's heart, and the reactions, on the part of others, of inertia, incomprehension, forgetfulness, ingratitude even, have not been foreseen. Those children can stay indifferent to the multiplied scoldings of their father and their mother ; the latter did not count their sacrifices to make Christians of them, and now they sadly find in their grown-up children the egoism that they had sacrificed in themselves.

How often have we heard the pessimistic reflections of quite generous Catholics who are worried about the sums squandered by the French Church in favour of Catholic schools—do the results, they ask us, repay so many sacrifices?

Add the deceptions of those who have boldly renounced their personal tranquility to occupy themselves, some with civic action, others with social or Catholic action. What mortification they have endured! Either their efforts have been abortive, or else, when they have succeeded even partially, their intentions have been regularly travested, and, in too many cases, their good will has been easily exploited.

There are some people who ask themselves whether the Christian order, which it is our sure mission to establish on earth, will ever be realised, whether it is even realisable. What is not the anguish of Catholics at the present time, who take Church doctrine seriously! We have the certainty that in the overturning of beliefs and of manners which no nation has escaped, we possess the only efficacious solution. The teaching of the Gospel interpreted and explained by the Popes and our theologians can—and is the only thing that can—bring order to spirits, settle social conflicts, establish concord in spite of the divergent interests of nations. But the world does not want to hear us. The voices of our leaders ring regularly against the conspiracy of silence, cleverly organised by those very people whom our doctrine would save and who are going to their ruin. Attention is only paid to programmes of violence and to preparations for war. Would we be reduced to tears, as was Jesus over his little earthly country, so hopelessly rebellious to His advances?

At the least, we need to turn towards Jesus Christ. like His Apostle, and say to Him " Lord, in spite of everything, we are still in the truth? Tell us that we are not fooling ourselves by making the sacrifice that you have asked of us in order to follow you? "

* * * *

It would be interesting, Brethren, to analyse Jesus' reply to Peter in detail with the variants in each of the three Evangelists. For lack of time, let us single out their essential traits.

The Lord makes a special promise to the Twelve. They themselves shall judge the twelve tribes of Israel. Then the Master addresses Himself, after them, to those who will have sacrificed all or part of their possessions and their dearest affections, for God's reign. To all, Jesus solemnly promises three things.

I.—*Eternal life, in the age to come.* This is the horizon of which the Christian ought never lose sight. We cannot go astray following in Jesus' foot-steps ; the indifference of the public, the apparent uselessness of our generosity, the failure of our attempts and even, if it had to come, our work falling to pieces, all that cannot destroy our union with God, that our life, on the contrary, makes more close every day and which will blossom out into eternal happiness with Him. Behind the defeat of Calvary, Jesus sees for us, as for Him, the splendours of Heaven. What will our fate be ? That of Jesus : suffering with Him and for Him, we will reign through Him and with Him [1].

We would be tempted no longer to turn back sadly, if we habitually kept our gaze towards eternity. The astonishing thing is not that we can relate everything to eternity, but that we neglect to do so, since it is for God's reign that we are giving our efforts and our sacrifices. Except only that we must not think of Heaven as the last *chance* of recompense for our present sufferings. " If I could be sure that this would be counted in my favour on high ! " Let us take a happy eternity as the first of the *certitudes.* Sure of victory, one does not spare one's pains, and one is not afraid of wounds.

---

[1] Rom., VIII, 17 ; II Tim., II, 12.

II.—But, before the certain rewards of the after-life, our Lord promises others to those who shall have renounced a legitimate good for His sake. Before " the heritage of everlasting life " they shall receive *now, in this world, a hundred times the worth of what they have sacrificed.*

Peter and his companions, among whom we notice uneasiness to-day, will recognise this immediately when, before giving Himself up to His death, Jesus will ask them : " Did you go in want of anything when I sent you out without purse, or wallet, or shoes ? They told him, nothing " [1]. Having cast off everything, they possessed nothing more. The Saviour sent them out without anything, yet they lacked nothing. What they sacrificed did not leave any defect in them.

But, here, Jesus is more affirmative still. He promises us a hundred times more than we lost on His account. Not evidently in material riches or sensible tenderness for there would be no sense here in talking of sacrifices any more, but rather of gross interests. The hunderfold that Jesus gives us, does not concern the quantity only of the joys that our pains ought to repay us; He will enhance the quality a hundred times.

The missionary, the Sister of Charity, have made plenty of sacrifices ; they have never ceased to be happy. In a pagan land, the missionary does recover a little homeland among the converted pagans. The Sister of Charity loves her sick like her own children. And without going as far as this total relinquishment you yourselves, Brethren, can attest that you have known your best joys in the privations that the love of Jesus Christ inspired in you. Alms that do not make us much poorer can remain a banal gesture, but when you give up some good for another's sake which would be useful to you, you feel yourself so much more united to God

---

[1] Luke, XXII, 35–36.

that you never regret what you have lost.

In the more intimate domain of conscience, can one compare the pleasures followed by torments with the peace of a life that keeps its unity ? If we forget ourselves in the spirit and the love of Christ, there is a hundred times more happiness in loving than in worrying about being loved, than in waiting for the always insufficient signs of friendship or in begging for an affection that is slipping away from us. There is a hundred times greater happiness in giving than receiving, in rendering service than in being served.

III.—Mark's text holds a surprise for us nevertheless. Jesus promises a singular reward here for those who leave all to follow Him. To eternal life in the world to come, and to happiness increased a hundredfold in the present life, the Master adds this strange favour : *persecutions !*

Jesus' thought remains constant. The last of the eight beatitudes had been " Blessed are those who are persecuted ". The happiness of following Jesus Christ, the faithful union with God, give the present life such sweetness that, by an unexpected counter-blow the Christian would end up by being too attached to the earth. Are there not besides, people who in order to deny the merit of good men, reproach them with the satisfaction they find in being good ? Under the injustice of this criticism, there is all the same a suspicion of truth ; one is so happy when one has been useful to someone ! The Saviour gets rid of this return of self-love, for us; " You shall receive the hundred fold of what you have given up, *but with persecution* ". And there we are cured of the egoistical dangers of vain glory or of the esteem of human praise. We shall receive ingratitude, in-comprehension and run the whole range of man's malice.

But even this trial is a reward. Let him not have enemies who wishes, it is said. Only the man, who possesses strength and valour is attacked. It is an honour to be numbered among those who are the butt of cowardice.

Then, seeing from whence the ridicule and the treachery, of which he is the victim, come, the Christian fully realises that these attacks are directed less against his own person than against Jesus whom he represents. What an honour to suffer for Him ! This joy ravished the first Apostles when, having been scourged by order of the Sanhedrin, they came out happy to have been judged worthy to suffer disgrace for the name of Jesus [1].

What of us, Brethren, who give all that we can to our Lord ? The fate of the Christian taking all in all, is the most enviable there is. He lacks for nothing who gives everything for the Gospel, when he possesses Jesus Christ. Let us repeat St. Thomas Aquinas' beautiful saying, when our Lord said to him " You wrote well about me, Thomas, what reward do you want ? .'— " Lord ", replied the saint, " none other than Yourself ".

---

[1] Acts, V, 41.

CHAPTER XIV

THE EXAMPLE OF FRATERNAL SERVICE.

Lord, is it for thee to wash my feet ?
(John XIII, 6.)

PETER and John at the Master's command had gone ahead to prepare the Paschal feast in a friend's house. When Jesus had joined them in the company of the other Apostles, a discussion arose among the latter: Which of them was to be accounted the greatest ? [1]

Were they still worrying about the places they would hold in the earthly kingdom which they still stubbornly hoped for, or was it a simple question of precedence about the order in which they should sit at table ? Their motives are not very important ; whatever they were, it must be stated sadly that on the very eve of the Saviour's death, their shabby preoccupations still keep them away from the doctrine that Jesus was teaching them for more than two years. They cannot tire the Saviour's patience. Once more, the Master reminds them that among the greatest disciples is the man who becomes the servant of all. " Tell me, which is greater ", He asks them " *the man who sits at table, or the man who serves him ?* "

Then the Apostles, already stretched out on the couches around the tables, see Him taking off His garments, putting a towel around Him, in order to begin the customary ablutions Himself. He pours water into a basin and kneels before Simon Peter in order to wash his feet.

Peter jumps up immediately. " It isn't possible ! " he protests, in terms in which we guess the sincere con-

[1] Luke, XXII, 24.

122

fusion that he feels. " *Lord, is it for thee to wash my feet ?* "
It is useless for Jesus to say that He will explain all to
him shortly, the Apostle will not let his Master debase
Himself to such an extent. " *I will never let thee wash
my feet !* " He is not speaking like this from obstinacy
but, loyally ; he cannot, nor his companions either, bear
Jesus forgetting who they are and who He is. Very
frankly but quite plainly Jesus replies to him. " *If I
do not wash thee, it means thou hast no companionship with
me !* No more is needed to swing him around completely.
Peter does not always grasp the Saviour's intentions,
but not to be His disciple any more, he would not have
that at any price ; and passing from one extreme to
the other, " *Then, Lord, wash my hands and my head too,
not only my feet !* " [1]

When Jesus has gone around all the tables, He says
to the Apostles. " *Do you understand what it is I have
done to you ? You hail me as the Master and the Lord ; and
you are right, it is what I am. Why then, if I have washed
your feet, I who am the Master and the Lord, you in your turn
ought to wash each other's feet ; I have been setting you an
example, which will teach you in your turn to do what I have
done for you*".

Peter understood this time even if the lesson were
addressed to all ; was it not concerned first of all with
him who was to receive the keys of the Kingdom ? All
will be obliged to obey the Head of the Church but
his authority will not be the exercise of a puerile or
tyrannical authority. The prerogative of the head is not
to receive the homage of his subordinates or to impose
his will arbitrarily on them, his role and its greatness
consist in serving these whom God has confided to him.
The greatest ought to respect the humblest, he is at
their service.

Later on Peter understood even better why Jesus

[1] John, XIII, 9.

wanted to kneel before Judas. There is not a single one of our brethren whom we are not bound to serve, whether they be the smallest or the most unworthy.

*   *   *   *

Is there any need, Brethren, to underline the immense import of this teaching of our Lord's ? It regulates the highest problems of social morality, as it guides us in the least daily contact with our equals.

In a way the lesson is two-fold. On the one hand, the authority in which the Christian rejoices commits him to *fraternal humility*. For all of us who have some authority, whether in the Church or the State, in the family, in a school, in the army, in an industry, a public office, everywhere that we are " greater " than our brothers, we must justify our situation by putting ourselves at the service of the least person there. The head ought to serve everywhere.

Under another aspect, Jesus' words also mean that a Christian's progress is only accomplished by the exercise of *fraternal service*. " You are great, therefore you ought to serve ". But also, " You would like to be great—for He is talking to men who are discussing their respective merits—you want to be great, you can, but to do it, you must serve ". Jesus does not give the casting vote in their pointless arguments. He does not settle who is the greatest. He, who was pleased to confuse the first and the last, did not set out any distinction between them and He cut the dispute short in a very definite manner ; the greatest becomes the servant of all.

" *Lord, is it for thee to wash my feet ?* " Peter is quite right to be amazed. Such a duty is not part of the ordinary attributes of a master. Jesus catches up on the Apostle's thought immediately. " I did not do this job *although* I am your Master ; it is *because* I am your Master and Lord, that I have washed your feet ". Then He continues : " The kings of the Gentiles lord it over them ; among the pagans, the chiefs only think of exercising their power over their inferiors. It is not to be like that for you. Amongst you, the head ought to be the one who serves, the greatest will be the servant of the others, like the example I have just given you ".

Here Jesus is promulgating the perfect Social Order. He is making a revolution in the age-old usages of mankind, where the strong have always been seen to enslave the weak, and the great to profit selfishly from the work and suffering of the small. Jesus gives us a completely different notion of authority. All authority comes from God and ought to tend, not to the advantage of those who hold it, but to the well-being of those over whom it is possessed. In the Christian plan, the Head is an intermediary between God and men, as Jesus, perfect head (*Christus caput Ecclesiae*), is also the Mediator *par excellence.*

From now on to serve will no longer be the humiliating condition of the small. The strong will have to respect and protect the weak. The great will have to put themselves at the service of the small. It is not that the roles are to be reversed, it is that they are better understood. Everybody ought to serve ; the man who commands and the one who obeys serve each other mutually, and together they serve God. This was indeed a revolution, a revolution of justice and of love.

But men can always be found to try and outdo Christ. They want to substitute for the Christian Order, a social order where there will be neither great nor little ; as there is " neither God nor Master " all men are equal. The inventors of these modern principles flatter themselves that they also have accomplished a revolution, without taking heed that they are merely bringing about a regression to the ancient slavery. One cannot establish a social order which is in opposition to the divine order of things.

In the Christian order, the relations between men are regulated by *fraternal humility ;* in the lay order, they are based on an *equality of pride.* Now, while Christian brotherhood tends to abolish progressively the artificial inequalities of human society and the social inequalities due to injustice, lay egalitarianism, on the contrary, only ends up in killing fraternity among men. The lay order pretends to deduce fraternity from equality : all men are equal therefore they are brothers. In Christianity the point of departure is not equality but fraternity ; because men are—not thanks to a symbolic title—but really brothers, this bond of blood, strengthened by the supernatural bond due to their divine sonship, creates a substantial equality between them and orders them to even out the differences that separate them. In contrast, the levelling egalitarianism cannot engender fraternity, it will always produce only rivals.

What is meant, in fact, when one speaks of equality among men ? At first sight men are so dissimilar. They are not endowed with the same health, with the same strength or with the same power to work. They are not all equally intelligent, ingenious, skilful. They have not all got the same tastes nor the same aptitudes. Their already different dispositions are not helped by equal luck—the land they must work is not equally rich ; fortune's goods are unfortunately scattered among all in unequal fashion.

However, human nature is one and every human being has an equal right to respect. In the human organism, all the members are equal and all ought to be cared for and honoured equally, but they do not possess the same importance because their functions are different. Thus humanity is one but the members of the social body are not uniform ; values like functions are necessarily in a hierarchy. This is why the levelling equality is anti-natural. It is an unrealisable dream. The levellings that came about in the cause of history have only given birth to new inequality, often more cruel than those preceding them. It is an unhealthy dream, for, at heart, many of those who clamour for it with difficulty disguise their ambitions for a superiority to which they could not attain otherwise. Inspired by envy, it is incapable of establishing love in the hearts of men.

The human order which Christianity bases on the brotherhood that equalises is completely different. Unequal among themselves by reason of the gifts they have received and the function they have to fulfil, men are equal before God. They have the same origin and the same divine destiny. Equal by nature, they are even more so because, all being redeemed by Jesus Christ, they are all called to possess the same divine life. " We all ", writes St. Paul, " have been baptised in a single Spirit, to form a single body . . . . there is no longer either Jew or Greek, or slave, or free man, you have all become one in Jesus Christ " [1].

Brothers in the same family have unequal qualities, but fraternal love, if it does not suppress the differences, makes an effort to wipe them out. In the great family of men, the family of which God is the Father, our Lord intends charity to equalise the different conditions and situations, to re-establish equilibrium in a spirit of equity. The greatest in fortune, in education, in knowledge, in the authority he enjoys, ought to put himself at the service of those to whom has fallen a less favourable or even unfortunate lot, just as Jesus, the Master and the Lord, washed the feet of His disciples.

---

[1] I Cor., XII, 13 ; Gal., III, 28.

The distinctions which exist between men ought no longer be, in a Christian society, a cause for division but rather become a means of drawing together. It will not be, as in the egalitarian revolution, the small who will drag down the great in order to take their places. In the fraternal revolution, the great, putting aside all pride, employ their superiority to raise up the humble. Between the egalitarianism which stirs up class-strife from below, and the despotism that keeps the class-struggle going from above (and the latter are no less fierce than the former) only fraternal humility can unite men equitably, as equally sons of God.

" *I have been setting you an example which will teach you in your turn to do what I have done for you* ". Jesus was not content just to show the Apostles the strict duty of leaders, He saw much farther. Not only will the greatest have to become the servant of his brothers, but all, forgetting whether they are great or small, will serve each other mutually. Everyone must devote himself to the service of all, and all must serve every individual person. Thus, serving each other, all will become great in the Kingdom of God. The Saviour said it so many times ; it is by humbling himself that man raises himself up.

The Christian will also have to watch out for the superiority of others over himself. We will joyfully offer the tribute of our obedience to those who have been placed by Providence over us. But even more than that, we will recognise that every man, whoever he is, surpasses us in some way. Assuredly in certain ways, this person or that is inferior to us, but the Christian does not stop there, he is only looking out for what he should respect, admire and imitate in others. St. Paul does not hesitate to formulate this rule. " Each of you must have the humility to think other men better than himself ".[1] In the Christian perspective, inferior

---

[1] Phil., II, 3.

situations do not make those who hold them inferior, these are just different situations where each person serves God and his brothers to the best of his ability. A man's real superiority does not lie in the task which is allotted to him, but in the manner in which he carries it out. To go even further, there is not a single one of our brethren who does not possess either a virtue or a talent that we lack, or at least, do not possess to the same degree. " Do not think yourself superior to others ", we read in the Imitation. " If you have any good quality, be persuaded that others possess in a finer manner. You will lose nothing by putting yourself lower than everybody, but if you put yourself over a single person, you are doing yourself a great wrong [1].

Humility is in reality an act of justice. It goes about seeking out and praising the good wherever it may be found. Through humility, we arrive at a truer feeling of human dignity and the respect we profess for others leads us straight into charity.

When we are on the watch-out to efface ourselves before the superiorities of others, we do not disregard the personal gifts that God has made, but we do, instead of being over-pleased with out merit, ask from modesty a sense of proportion, a consciousness of our limits. Also, without ever trying to impose ourselves on others, we are always disposed to give them the benefit of the advantages we possess and they lack.

Men have a tendency to guard their privileges jealously. What they possess in common with others seems to be less estimable than what they have on their own. To have what others have not, to know what others are ignorant of, to be able to do what is impossible for them is, in their eyes, a good so much more precious because others lack it, and they do not want to part with it either ! What is their good is the real good.

[1] Imit., book I, ch. 7, no. 3.

Jesus teaches us, on the contrary, that the loveliest privilege is to be able to serve, to want to give and to know how to share.

Are we the " least ", whom others often need ? In helping them, we contribute to their greatness, we raise them up. And if we are the " greatest ", we do not lower ourselves by bending down to one of our brothers, we only stoop to raise him up with us, by bringing ourselves back up with him.

Let us imitate the Master's example faithfully. He did not consider He lost rank by washing His Apostle's feet. Let us make it our aim to grow to the height of the Son of Man who " came not to be served, but to serve ".

CHAPTER XV

THE LESSONS OF A FAULT :

FROM GENEROSITY TO PRESUMPTION

I am ready to lay down my life for thy sake !—
Thou art ready to lay down thy life for my sake ?
Believe me, by cock-crow thou wilt thrice disown me.

(John, XIII, 37–38.)

SIMON PETER'S sad adventure is one of the most familiar themes for the reflection of Christians. It is a truly instructive example for our weakness, but fitting also for raising us from discouragement. This is no doubt why the head of the Apostles wanted his mishap to be related throughout the first Christian preaching, of which our Gospels are a resumé.

In making a very humble avowal of his fault to the whole church, Peter also found the occasion to renew unceasingly the expression of his repentance to his beloved Master. Without wanting to, he also reveals in this the most admirable riches of his generous nature.

But Peter had the right to humiliate himself at the memory of his error, we certainly do not have the right to be scornful about it. Our duty is to use the lessons of his fault.

Would those who let themselves censure him without any leniency have had more courage in his place ? In any case, they would not have had as much love for Jesus. As an epigraph for this meditation and those following, I will put the otherwise exact appreciation that St. Jerome gives of the Apostle, who is ready to die rather than deny his Master. "There is neither temerity nor falsehood ", he writes, " attached to Peter, but an act of faith and an ardent love for the Saviour " [1].

*   *   *   *

The announcement of his denial that Jesus makes to Peter, is reported by the four evangelists with variations that complement one another. To-day we will study St. John's narrative. In briefer form, it allows us to grasp the true feelings of the Apostle quite well and the initial mistake that must have brought about his downfall.

Our Lord after having explained to the Apostles the meaning of the act which He had performed when He washed their feet, denounced the one among them who would betray Him. Judas left the guest chamber. The meal over, Jesus instituted the sacrament of His love. The hour of His departure is near and His own people will find Him again in the Eucharist. Let them always remain united among themselves ! The Saviour begs them to love each other as He has loved them ; this is the sign by which they will be recognised as His disciples.

Simon Peter has listened religiously to this urgent exhortation to fraternal charity. But something weighs him down : the Master is going to disappear. " *Lord* ", he asks Him, " *where are you going ?* " Let us spare the Apostle the accusation of a perfectly inadmissible dullness of spirit. Jesus has said too clearly that He is leaving them the sacrament of His body " which will be delivered up for them ", of His blood, " which will be shed for them and for many ". Peter can no longer cherish the least doubt : Jesus must die. But what is death for the Son of God, and in what circumstances shall it come about ? All the same Peter is not going to abandon

[1] *Non est temeritas nec mendacium : sed fides est apostoli Petri, et ardens affectus erga Dominum Salvatorem.*

the Lord in this tragic moment.

Jesus replies : " *I am going where thou canst not follow me now, but shalt follow me afterwards* ".

The Apostle's reply is immediate, it is what it ought logically, it seems, to be. Why later ? " *Lord, why cannot I follow thee now ? I am ready to lay down my life for thy sake* ". He has a good idea then of the drama that is going to be unfolded. Jesus is talking about violent death. There will therefore be a struggle to be undergone. And Peter will not be there to defend Him . . . ! He will shield Him with his body . . . .

The wish of all who love springs forth from the vibrant heart of the Apostle. Rather than see Jesus die, he would gladly die in His place ! Or if he cannot substitute his own death for the Master's then he would die *with* Him. To live on when Jesus would be dead ! But what would he do on earth ? In the Apostle's cry, there is no pride, there is only love.

What emotion, what sweetness must have invaded the Heart of Jesus at this moment ! It would be a complete misrepresentation of the Saviour's character, it would set Him beneath his disciple to imagine that Peter's spontaneous, sincere, overflowing affection would only produce from Him the cold, distant lesson of a disabused moralist. No, there is neither scepticism nor deception in Jesus' reply. If we are listening to it, let us try to divine the accent of the man who is speaking. If we are reading it, let us contemplate the two speakers, let us observe their looks meeting over two abysses of tenderness.

Jesus does not refuse His Apostle's sacrifice. He has just said to him : " Not now, not yet. Later ". Peter will certainly follow him. But before that he must take up the leadership of the Church, the Kingdom of

God, the keys of which have been confided to him. Jesus' mission is come to an end ; Peter's is only beginning. It would be too beautiful to be able to go off with those one loves. One loves them more by surviving them in order to continue their work. Peter will rejoin the Saviour certainly. But not immediately, rather, when he will be full of merit, when his faith will be stronger, as strong as his present love, when this affection shall have reached higher degrees still. " *Thou art ready to lay down thy life for my sake ?* " Jesus answers. I know well, Peter, that you are capable of it, but you must, before you die for me, learn to suffer for my sake and that is much more difficult. " *Believe me, by cockcrow,* my poor Peter, *thou wilt thrice disown me* ".

We will examine now the text of the Synoptic Gospel, and particularly the sentence where Peter seems to be professing to be stronger than the others. Will we stop for a moment at the first dialogue between the Master and His disciple. I have been unable, I have not succeeded in finding either harshness in the Saviour's attitude or the slightest ostentation in Peter's. I only see an affection without bounds, on both sides. But Peter's love has gone involuntarily astray and Jesus' love puts it back in order.

*　　*　　*　　*

" I am ready to lay down my life for thy sake ! " *Non est temeritas nec mendacium.* Peter is not making a promise in the air. His resolution, to die for Jesus, is sincere. When it comes to a show-down, he will not slink away. When the high-priest's emissaries come to arrest Jesus in the garden of Olives, Peter faces them boldly ; he unsheaths, and with a blow of his sword, he slices the ear of one of the scoundrels who were hurling themselves at Jesus. He would have continued to strike if Jesus had not formally forbidden him. He was therefore ready to receive blows and wounds for Jesus and to be killed for Him. We might note, in parenthesis, that the Synoptics are carefully silent about the name of the disciple who drew his sword to defend Jesus. Peter's humility had doubtless demanded it. When St. John wrote his Gospel, the head of the Roman Church had been dead for a long time ; there was no longer any reason to keep him anonymous.

Peter had therefore spoken truly : he was ready to die for Jesus. But Jesus had also spoken truly : before cock-crow Peter declared three times that he did not know Him at all.

One would need never to have studied oneself to show surprise that the Apostle, capable of sacrificing his life, should have given way before poor jokes. We ourselves, Brethren, are sincere when we affirm to God that we love Him above everything. Above everything ! And we then refuse Him the sacrifice of the tiniest pleasure. We are not lying : we would be ready, if it were necessary to die in order to affirm our faith ; and then we hide it in order to avoid being made fun of or we forget Him when one of His light rules inconveniences us. Ought we then to abstain from reciting our " act of charity ", and was Peter wrong to declare, " I am ready to lay down my life for thy sake " ?

St. Jerome did not think so. No, Peter is not fool-hardy when he makes an offering of his life to the Lord. Jesus asked it of him. He asks it of all His disciples ; we ought to love Him more than our riches, than our parents, more than ourselves. We will only save our life if we consent to losing it for Him. And it is this total gift that the Apostle makes Him. In presenting it to Him in all the rapture of his loving will, Peter does not sin through an excess of boldness.

His mistake—and ours—is to make *promises* which are not, at the same time, a *prayer*. We are ambitious, but will never be enough so in the service of Jesus Christ, our desire to love Him, we saw it lately, ought not recognise any limits. Now, if we only count on ourselves to put this desire into execution, we immediately shut our generosity up in the narrow limits of human weakness. Peter *presumed* about his strength, in which he was mistaken. He was strong enough to let himself be killed, but not enough to stand up to the jokes of the guard-room.

Jesus Christ wants our desire to love Him to be immense, our ambitions to holiness to be immense, the projects of our apostolate to be immense. But the desires of the Christian ought, at the same time, to be a prayer. Everywhere we meet the imprescriptible rule of the Gospel : " He, who exalts himself will be humbled, he who humbles himself will be exalted ", for it is Christ alone who can make us great.

St. Phillip Neri composed for himself as a litany of ejaculatory prayers, short epigrams of humility which contain, at the same time, the conditions of efficacious action. He did not dare say " My God, I love you ", he said, " I will never love you sufficiently if you do not help me, my Jesus . . . . I have never loved you and I want so much to love you . . . . . If you do not help me, I shall fall, my Jesus ". And this one is just as beautiful, " Lord, beware of me who will betray you and do you every wrong imaginable, if you do not come to my aid " [1].

This is how our holy ambitions, emptied of the presumption that makes them sterile, are expressed. We can neither progress nor maintain our progress, if we forget our " insufficiency " or, to use St. Paul's expression, if we are not convinced that " all our ability

---

[1] Father Olivaint, no doubt inspired by St. Phillip said : " Lord, be on Your guard against me, for if You do not watch out, I will betray You to-day ".

comes from God " [2]. " It is by the grace of God, that I am what I am ". And if he can write (for humility does not oblige him to bring himself into disrepute or to deny the evidence) " I have worked harder than all of them " he quickly adds, " or rather, it was not I, but the grace of God working with me " [2]. He also found, not in his works or his visions, but only in his weaknesses, in the really experienced feeling of his insufficiencies, a subject of glory, not for himself obviously, but for Jesus Christ who made good his deficiencies.

With Jesus, we can do everything; that is what justifies our ambitions—but let us have a good strong conviction of our insufficiency for " without me ", the Master says to us, " you can do nothing ".

We will offer ourselves therefore, completely. But to offer oneself to someone is essentially to put oneself at his disposal. In offering ourselves to God without reserve, we will, in consequence, argue that He takes from us all that He wants, but only what He wants. He alone, besides, knows of what we are capable.

Peter's generous promise was not only marked with *presumption*, it lacked discretion. Before Peter could die for Jesus, Jesus had to die for Peter. Our Peter, always jealous, was going ahead without taking heed of the designs of Providence. Jesus put him gently back on the path marked out by God : not now, " *thou shalt follow me afterwards* ". Afterwards, in fact, Peter will undergo the same punishment as His Saviour. Before letting him die for Him, Jesus wants Peter to learn how *to live* for Him, *to work* for Him. Before being bound with fetters, he must bind himself to his daily task and learn to suffer for Him. Before suffering the blows of the executioner's hammer, he will have to endure the Sanhedrin's birches and, before the blows of the whip,

[1] II Cor., III, 5.
[2] I Cor., XV, 10.

he must learn " this very night " to conquer the pin-pricks of irony and the jeering glances of a servant-girl.

Holiness is not reached in a single leap, one only gets there progressively, by stages—*per gressus*. One step after the other, with a fall often between two. Peter had to have that cruel experience : " *by cock-crow thou wilt thrice disown me* ".

This experience of the Apostle's, have we not all had it, and quite often too ? One throws oneself madly into action, one adopts a crude discipline to reform one's character, one takes on, without due consideration, too many pious obligations, just to give in, alas, at the first little temptation that comes one's way. Providence has made it its business to recall discretion to our minds.

There is no uniform sanctity or sanctification. We all have a special vocation. God calls us to a perfection, which He Himself points out to each of us, and for which He gives each of us proportionate knowledge and help. We will only reach this perfection in the place assigned to us by Providence, with the aid of the means given us by Providence, and in the time willed by God. Whoever wanders from the plan that God has conceived for him because he wants to do too much—because he wants to copy another's holiness—because he wants to " crash the lights ", inevitably puts him in danger of falling back instead of advancing. He is the victim, not of his desire for perfection but of his indiscreet illusions.

How many mothers of families go astray because they try to force their lives to a spiritual régime which imitates that of monasteries ! There is a lay perfection as there is a religious perfection. Lay perfection does not consist in copying what is the perfection of the convent, without ever succeeding either, or else one would have to say that Christianity is only for a minority of the faithful—for the minority which does not lead the ordinary life of the rest of the world. Christianity would no longer be the religion of everybody—the Catholic religion. We can make ourselves holy in every situation in which God places us, and therefore we can do so in family life, looking after the home and the children, in our workshop or at our work-table. The Carthusian sanctifies himself in contemplation and St. Joseph became holy at his bench. The Carmelite in fasting and the mother in bringing well-being and joy to her home. Wherever God has placed you, in your home, your office, in your social circle, you have a fixed task to perform—it is not your neighbour's, it is yours—and according to God's intention, it ought to sanctify you if, there where you are, you live your Christianity to the full. Where God has put you, you are irreplaceable, you are given an apostolate that no one else but you can discharge. Do not look for another field of action, it is there that you will sanctify yourself by making your brethren holy.

" You are ready to lay down your life for Jesus ! " Of course, Christians, but do not lose your sense of reality, give your life as God has done for you. Do not offer Him what He has not asked of you at all ; find out, rather, what He expects from your education, your condition, your trade, your state of health, the time you can spare, your natural temperament. Be content with the humble duties, the poor occupation, the obscure mortification that He imposes on you. Give Him (without hesitating) all that He demands, not from others, but from you and let Him, at His own pleasure, increase the amount of your renunciations, the extent of your shining influence, and your chances of mortification. Christ asks us to follow Him, not to go before Him. St. Vincent de Paul, observing that Our Lord had not accomplished the half of the works that His divine power would have allowed Him to do, drew this moral from it : " Let us honour this divine Master, especially in the moderation of His action. He did not want always to do what He could have done, in order to teach us to be satisfied when it is not expedient to do all that we might do ".[1] Discretion, sobriety, a sense of proportion, these capital virtues keep us within the limits willed by Providence, and outside which progress and perfection are impossible.

There was certainly an immense love in Peter's enthusiastic gallantry : " *I am ready to lay down my life for thy sake* ". And yet Jesus received a greater love still from His disciple after his denial, love arising from the humility which followed his fault, from the sadness of his repentance and the joy of the forgiveness he received.

May our generosity towards our Lord never make us forget, Brethren, that yesterday we were sinners and we can fall to-morrow again, for we are always weak. Do not let us give the Lord what we are dreaming about but what He asks of us, asking Him ourselves to help us not to refuse Him . . . " Lord, be on your guard against me, for if you do not watch out, I will betray you to-day ".

---

[1] Abelly, 1., III, ch. 16.

CHAPTER XVI

JESUS' PRAYER FOR SINNERS.

I have prayed for thee, that thy faith may not fail ;
when after a while thou hast come back to me, it is
for thee to be the support of thy brethren.

(Luke XXII, 32–34. Parallel passages :
Matt. XXVI, 31–35 ; Mark XIV, 27–31).

In contrast to St. John and St. Luke the first two Gospels
do not place the announcement of Peter's denial inside
the Supper-Room, but on the road leading to Mount
Olivet. The three Synoptics introduce it, however, in
the same way, so that where in St. John it is the desire
to follow Jesus to His death that leads Simon Peter
astray, the first three evangelists present his protestation
as a reply to Jesus' first prophesy, foretelling the general
desertion of the Apostles. " *To-night you will all lose
courage over me* ", the Master said to them, and to lessen
the terrible effect of this warning, He adds that their
desertion was foreseen by the prophet " *I will smite the
shepherd and the sheep of his flock will be scattered* ". Besides,
their unfaithfulness will not last long for they will gather
together once more around Him in Galilee after His
Resurrection.

St. Luke's text is more touching. Jesus speaks directly
to Peter, but from delicacy He does not give him his
new name. To call him " Rock " just when He is
speaking to him of his approaching inconstancy would
be too cruel an irony. He addresses him by his proper
name, as we say to-day, his Christian name, which gives

the Saviour's sentence a more affectionate touch,
" *Simon, Simon, behold Satan has claimed power over you
all, so that he can sift you like wheat !* " The Apostles'
desertion will not be final, but they are going to be
shaken by temptation like the grain tossed in the winnowing basket.

When they hear these words, the eleven Apostles are
already depressed by the sorrow and indignation that
Judas' treachery caused them. Jesus told John and
Peter what the wretch was up to, now all knew why
the Treasurer had left the guest-chamber so suddenly.
Was one traitor not enough then ? Does Jesus mean to
say that the others will go over to the enemy or that
they will flee like cowards.

They cry out with one voice, but Peter, the most
impetuous of all, speaks first. " *Lord, I am ready to bear
thee company though it were to prison or to death*". St.
Matthew and St. Mark note that *all the rest of His
disciples said the like*. So all, without exception, boast
that they are ready to go to prison or to death. But the
two evangelists put a declaration in Peter's mouth that
scarcely surprises us on the part of this incorrigible and
impulsive man, and which makes the Saviour tell him
that before cock-crow he will have denied Him three
times. " *Though all else should lose courage over thee, I will
never lose mine*".

Should this reply of the Apostle deserve more severity
from us ? Let us beware of condemning him too quickly,
for we would fall in our turn into the fault into which
he fell so unthinkingly.

To judge him fairly one must not forget that Peter
was broken-hearted over the close death of his Master
and over Judas' crime. He has some excuse therefore
for not being calm. He loves Jesus to the point of
madness, he is His for life, to the death. He cries out

to Him with all the force of his tenderness " Though all else should lose courage over thee, I will never lose mine ". He could not speak for the others, but he could for himself, " *Etsi omnes, ego non !* "

There is fire clustering in Peter's exclamation ! Is it not the mark of men of character to look for their rule of conduct in their consciences only, and not only not to be worried by opinions or by the majority but to find in the capitulation of others an even greater reason to remain attached to their ideal and not to yield in their resolution ?

When all will deny Jesus Christ, I won't ! This is the same sentiment that gave the Church her glorious crown of martyrs ! *Etsi omnes, ego non !* It is certainly quite pardonable to surrender to an enemy superior in number which surrounds you on all sides, when you can do nothing more against him. And yet, " a French officer never surrenders " Lieutenant Gaëtan de Kainlis cried before Verdun, offering his breast to the German bayonets. *Etsi omnes, ego non !* This is a hero's speech ! It is the speech of generous natures, of those who attack the injustices from which they wish to deliver suffering humanity. When all others are silent before abuses, the man of heart will always want to proclaim the truth ! *Etsi omnes, ego non !* Peter's speech is the speech of a brave man !

On second examination, however, it must be admitted that it is quite humiliating for his companions in the group of Apostles. He is not answerable for the others, of course, but, nonetheless, he accepts the supposition that the other Apostles could abandon Jesus, which is tantamount to saying, at least by deduction, that he is superior to them.

It seems, indeed, that, at the time of the apparition on Lake Tiberias Jesus, in asking Simon if he loved Him " more than the others ", gave rise to an illusion close to the mistake he makes by asserting that he will never fail Him, even if the others should do so. And besides Peter knew how not to relapse into error.

He made his mistake then in believing himself capable of resisting when the others would succomb. But one must allow him that he only imagined the failure of the others hypothetically. In the case of the others failing, he, at least, would not fail. In reality, Peter is thinking less of the other's case than his own. His fault is the one we considered before, a presumptuous confidence in himself. It is only, it seems, indirectly— by accident—that he maligns the others. So great was his presumption, besides, that not only did he, without thinking, place himself above the others, but he arrived at the stage of not believing that the Master's word could be realised. He doubts Jesus rather than doubt himself.

Now (this is where the lesson takes on its full meaning) Peter would not have doubted Jesus if he had known how to doubt himself, and he would have been less blind to his own true worth if he had remembered that a disciple of Christ's ought to place himself spontaneously lower than all his brethren. His premier fault is presumption which always arises from a lack of humility.

" We are all weak ", writes the author of the Imitation, " but be sure that no one is weaker than yourself " [1]. St. Francis of Assisi was not afraid to place himself beneath all sinners. He held to this reasoning. " If God had given this sinner as much as He has given thee, this brigand would be holier than thou ! " On the contrary, we quickly become presumptious as soon as we compare ourselves to those who seem more imperfect than us. The worst punishment of the proud— and they do not always have long to wait for it—is to fall into the fault for which they have criticized others

---

[1] *Imit.*, bk. I, ch. 2, no. 4.

severely. None of the eleven Apostles wishes to admit that he will be a deserter and all abandoned Jesus. Peter was sure that he, in any case, would stand firm and he added his denial to the general flight.

If they had only remained in the prudent doubt that they showed when Jesus told them that one among them was a traitor ! How touching their humility was then ! Not a single one looked in Judas' direction not a single one suspected his brethren, none of them jumped up at the thought of being accused of such a crime. But all were miserable, as if each of them could have been a traitor. One after another, they had said to Jesus, " Master, is it I ? Is it I, Lord ? " The sin into which we fall is often that of which we considered ourselves incapable, and one avoids it most surely when one has the conviction that one would be capable of committing it. A feeling of our own weakness makes us prudent and have recourse to prayer. " It is when I feel myself weak that I am strong " wrote St. Paul. The reverse is no less true. We are never as frail as when we blind ourselves about our strength.

* * * *

If we do not have the right to show ourselves severe on Simon Peter, it is not only because we have revived his fault so often. A more powerful reason forbids us. We observe, in fact, that our Lord, while foretelling that His Apostle will disown Him, does not add any reproach to this said declaration. We heard Jesus speaking to him severely for the least failings. Here, one would almost be tempted to ask whether the fault were not forgiven before being committed. There will be so little malice in Peter's sin, and he will suffer so dreadfully for it, that the Saviour seems to be pre-

occupied above all with keeping up his courage after
he will have failed Him.

Listen how He speaks to the future sinner, with what
care He confirms him in advance in his role as head.
It is no longer the majestic enthronement of " *Tu es
Petro* " but a sermon of farewell, just as categorical and
more poignant. And the Council of the Vatican has
taken over these words that Jesus addresses to the Apostle
who is going to sin, to support the definition of the
doctrinal infallibility of his successors. " *I have prayed
for thee that thy faith may not fail ; when, after a while,
thou hast come back to me, it is for thee to be the support of thy
brethren* ". We look for a reproach, we only find a
promise, " I have prayed for Thee ! . . . .

In other circumstances, Peter would, without doubt,
have thrown himself at Jesus' feet, as he did after the
miraculous draught of fishes. He would have said,
" Oh, do, Lord, pray for me, for I am a sinner ! " But
he only hears Jesus through his emotion, much as one
listens to holy souls who promise their prayers in times
of trial. One thanks them from politeness without
being quite sure what they have been saying. Peter is
too worked up to calculate on the spot what would be
the worth of Jesus' prayer for him. He will remember
it later, and this memory will save him from despair.

" *I have prayed for thee !* " Jesus prayed for Peter and
Peter fell. There are few things in the Gospel so en-
couraging for sinners such as ourselves; it is not to prevent
Peter's fall that Jesus prayed, it is, knowing that he
will fall, that he may raise himself up again immediately.
Jesus does not say : " I have prayed that thy firmness
may not waver ". He did not demand a courage from
his disciple that his very presumption made impossible.
Prayer, even that of the Son of God, will never negative
our liberty. " *I have prayed* ", says the Saviour " *that
thy faith may not fail* ". Peter will be embarrassed about

Jesus, but, in the depths of his heart, he will not deny Him. Certainly his fault will be a great misfortune, but it would be even greater if he did not rally from it. God always makes good come out of evil. He will make His disciple's sin serve the plans of His mercy. Peter's faith will not collapse under this test, it will rise out of it, strengthened, invincible henceforward, and what is more, conquering.

" *I have prayed for thee, that thy faith may not fail !* " It will waver nonetheless. Peter will not stop loving his Master passionately for an instant, but an eclipse will pass over his spirit. How could he and his companions have stood firm against such stupefying events ? Jesus condemned by the religious authorities, Jesus reduced to helplessness, not defending Himself any more, Jesus apparently abandoned by God whom He called His Father ! . . . . . The Saviour knows that their faith will drift and He anticipates them. But Peter's faith will not be wrecked.

But when the women bring the angel's message to the guest-room on Easter Sunday morning, Peter does not go against the opinion of the other Apostles, who count the women's story as an absurdity. All the same, he wants to see for himself at the tomb, his faith has not disappeared, a never-ending hope still struggles inside him in spite of the brutal evidence of the facts. You see, Jesus had prayed for Peter. The disciple's *courage* had failed, not *his love,* and his charity safeguarded his *faith.* Peter knew the mortal anxieties of the soul which wants to believe all the more strongly because it cannot articulate its belief. Terrible hours when one clasps desperately at the beloved God who seems to be avoiding our grasp. Interior dreams when we would have foundered if Jesus had not prayed for us. The torturing nights that seemed to be years ! The Christian, whom the Lord does not spare from these torments of darkness ought not think that his faith has deserted him. His faith will never, perhaps, have been more powerful or more active than during these frightful hours. To believe is not to see. The touch-stone of faith is, on the contrary, that in these sad crises you continue to say "Yes", even when you only see "No". We will never perhaps love God for Himself as much as when our poor soul, deprived of light, emptied of joy, the prey of a giddiness similar to that caused by physical starvation, hears nothing more than the echo of its own distress. Far from failing, however, our love becomes stronger after it has passed through the burning crucible of incertitude. It is then that it seizes us without our knowledge, and it penetrates us till from now on it will be inseparable from our spirit.

What goods do we hold on to hardest in this world, indeed, but those which we acquired by means of work, of struggles, of sacrifices ? After that they belong to us and we can distribute them among other people.

Among the temptations that assail us, what strength we draw from the certitude that Jesus prayed for us ! From that alone, this thought can give us the victory. When the temptation is so violent that we imagine we feel ourselves in our turn being shaken by a winnowing fan, what courage we will get in recalling that the Lord will make us rise out of this crisis with an increased virtue, and with new possibilities of being a support for our brethren.

This is how Peter's faith must have been. " *When thou hast come back to me, it is for thee to be the support of thy brethren.*" Simon Peter had to go through all that to become a support for his brethren. After this sorrowful experience he will be the unshakeable foundation of the whole Church. He will be able then to present himself to others and reassure them ; will they doubt that the Lord will forgive them, when He forgave him, he who was more guilty than they?

Peter praised himself, " *Though all else should lose courage over thee, I will never lose mine!*" It would indeed have been a splendid miracle to see the leader of the Apostles escape the general disaster. Jesus reserved another privilege for him, that of raising up his brethren, after he had fallen lower than any of them. Peter will disown Him three times in the space of an hour, but he will have all his life to disown his denial. And for a long time after he shall have left this earth, as long as the Church will last, the example of his conversion will strengthen Christians, not only the example of his conversion, but the certainty that this conversion was due to the prayers of Jesus Christ.

God's plan will not suffer from his triple weakness. The whole Church rests on Peter, but Peter cannot waver because Jesus prayed for him that his faith might not fail. Till the end of time, Christians will turn to the head of the Church, sure of finding in him the indefectible faith of Peter.

CHAPTER XVII

PRAYER AND VIGILANCE

*Simon, art thou sleeping ?   Hadst thou not the
strength to watch even for an hour ?*

(Mark XIV, 37.   Parallel passages :
Matt. XXVI, 36–43 ; Luke XXII,
40–46).

ST. MARK is the only one to blame Peter alone for
disappointing Jesus. In the two other Synoptic Gospels
Jesus' reproach is addressed to His companions also.
He is speaking to the three privileged ones, to those
whom He brought into the room when He raised Janus'
daughter, the three witnesses of His glory on the mountain
of the Transfiguration.

Once he had arrived at Gethsemani, Jesus sent the
other Apostles a stone's throw away, bringing Simon,
James and John with Him. He had confided to them
the mortal sadness of His soul and the anguish with
which His whole body trembled at the moment of the
bloody fulfilment of our Redemption. Of course, He
had only come down to earth for this hour, but that
made it no less terrible. " *Do you abide here* ", He said
to them, " *and keep watch* ". Then He went forward a
few steps and fell on the ground. The three disciples
heard His sorrowful prayer, it was always the same words
that came back again and again through His sighs :
" *Father, all things are possible to thee ; take away this
chalice from before me . . .   Only as thy will is, not as mine is* ".

It is impossible to think that the Apostles did not
cry out at first like their Master and that they did not
join their prayers to His. But soon the stillness, the
darkness of the night, tiredness, stupefied them and their

eyes grew heavy. St. Luke, with the professional observation of the doctor, points out another reason for their sleepiness : sorrow. Their eyes scalded with tears, could no longer stay open. Before the incomprehensible drama at which they were assisting their emptied brain could no longer hold a single thought and their heads drooped in spite of themselves.

And when Jesus, broken by the struggle going on in His heart, interrupted His prayer and came over to His disciples, He found them asleep.

One can easily imagine their shame when the Saviour's voice woke them ! They, chosen from the others, how did they feel about not being able to support their Master in His suffering ! Peter, telling of this sad episode in his preaching later on, felt such sorrow about it that he took on himself alone the affectionate chiding of the Lord. This is doubtless why St. Mark, whose Gospel simply transcribes Peter's recitation, only mentions him, " *Simon, art thou sleeping ? Hadst thou not the strength to watch even for an hour ?* "

As usual, St. Luke's narrative is more concise. Jesus only intervenes once, " *How can you sleep ? Rise up and pray so that you may not enter into temptation!* " But the first two Evangelists wanted to be sure we knew that in spite of His first warning, while Jesus went back to pray, repeating, alas, the same words of poignant sorrow and total abandonment to the divine will all the time, the three Apostles yielded once more to the physical and moral dejection that kept them from staying awake.

Brethren, we have more to do than to be scandalised at their relapse. Their prostration justifies only too well the aptness of the lesson that Jesus gives them, so gently, in the middle of His agony and which applies equally to us all, " *The spirit is willing enough but the flesh is weak* ". It is not by the generosity of our desires that our fervour is measured. As long as we have not translated them into actions, our desires are only words. At the moment of making promises, our good will may quite well be whole-hearted, but will it be able to go against the repugnance or the opposition of our too feeble nature ? For to obey the spirit, the help of divine grace is necessary, " *Watch and pray, that you may not enter into temptation* ".

*　　*　　*　　*

The word " temptation " is taken here, as in many passages of Scripture, in its first and more general sense of a " *trial or test* ". " Blessed is he who endures under trials ", writes St. James, " When he has proved his worth, he will win the crown of life ". *Beatus vir qui suffert tentationem* [1]. Before leaving the supper chamber, Our Lord congratulated and thanked the Apostles for having stayed with Him during His hours of trial. " *Vos estis qui permansistis mecum* in tentationibus *meis* " [2].

But as our virtue is exposed to personal or exterior events that turn us from good or attract us to evil, in common usage, the word " temptation " has come to mean, not only persecution or affliction, but, more usually, the inclination to evil, a *moral trial*.

Whether it is a trial arising out of outside events or the difficulty of practising virtue, in both cases, faithfulness must be proven. The conditions for success are the same : not to let ourselves be swept away by enthusiastic desires or grandiose promises, but to remember that we are beings of flesh and blood, very frail, and condemned to failure without divine co-operation. " *Watch and pray !* "

This double precaution is indispensable, according to the Master, so as not " to enter into temptation ". This expression does not mean that those who watch and

---

[1] James, I, 12.
[2] Luke, XXII, 28.

pray, will be spared affliction or even repugnance to their duty. Was not our Lord Himself, at the moment He was proclaiming this law, being subjected to the cruellest of trials, and the most violent of temptations ? " *Take away this chalice from before me* . . . . . " But the Saviour avoids the tempter's snares properly. He does not fall into the error to which our weak human nature, always fleeing from suffering, drags us ; He does not accept the point of view of the flesh, He frees the spirit from its grip, " *Father, only as Thy will is, not as Mine is !* " not the flesh, but the Spirit ! Jesus watches and prays and He does not enter into temptation, that is to say, He does not succumb to it.

To go still further, as far as we are concerned, vigilance and prayer will do nothing to keep us from being tempted or put to trial. Temptation is inevitable, a trial is necessary. But from whence will we draw the strength to resist them ? Jesus teaches us from whence, it is not in giving ourselves over to too vivid an imagination (*spiritus quidem promptus est*) it is not in believing ourselves strong, but, on the contrary, in never losing the feeling of our weakness (*caro autem infirma*). We will avoid discouragement as we will sin by keeping on our guard and by praying. One cannot pray and sin at the same time. Whoever has a spirit that is strongly attached to God cannot, at the same time, push away the chalice and say to the Father, " *Not Thy will* . . . "

Once more, we must get our Lord's advice exactly right: Watch *and* pray, and not to separate these two means, for it is only their combination that assures our success. The vigilance which warns us of danger does not alone protect us from it. It is exactly the opposite, the clearer our view of the peril, the more timid and vulnerable we would become. And by itself prayer is, likewise, not enough. We would wait in vain for the help of Heaven if we did not flee the occasions of evil, if we did not repress the flaws in our make-up, if we did not employ all our natural energies. Watch *and* pray. The two duties are complementary and is it not because they are inseparable that our Lord had first put them together as one in the even simpler formula " *Watch with Me* " ? With Him, near Him, prayer keeps us awake, and vigilance is a prayer.

" *Had you no strength then to watch an hour with Me ?* " We need not doubt that the three disciples began by praying. But to pray for an hour when one is worn out with fatigue and overcome with sorrow is a lot to demand from our too feeble flesh. They were certainly determined to stay awake so as to get up at the first warning, the proof is that Peter was holding a sword in his hand. But it is difficult to remain alone in the face of one's thoughts, without stirring, in the silence, in the night . . . .

Oh ! If they had repeated the suppliant prayer that they heard falling from their Master's lips, without attempting more ! Maybe they were not able to watch for an hour, because they were thinking of themselves rather than of Him ! If they had only tried to share the sorrow and anguish of the Divine sufferer, the dismay of the Author of life, hanging on the brink of death, the disgust of His most pure heart, invaded by the horrible irruption of all human villainy ! Their spirit would not have been so inconstant then ; they would have conquered the fatigue of the flesh if they had associated themselves more closely to the suffering and prayer of Jesus. They would not have abandoned Him later, if they had known how to watch with Him . . . Brethren, since the best of the Apostles could not stop themselves from slumbering—not from indifference but from simple weakness—let us endeavour to understand, as they did not, the full force of these three words : " *Watch with Me !* " These three words promise us

salvation in our moral difficulties and courage in all
the trials of life.

I.—So that temptation may not lead us to sin, let us
watch our weak points attentively, let us restrict ourselves
to a programme of life which keeps us from the dangers
of incoherence, and the tricks of fantasy, do not let us
forgive our negligences, let us control severely the influences to which we are subjected. These measures
of vigilance are of the highest importance. One must
only want to take them and to want to always, without
growing tired. But this continuity of effort, alone
capable of making vigilance efficacious, supposes a
strength that, as a general rule, surpasses the ordinary
powers of human nature.

We will then need to unite prayer with vigilance. A
prayer of intense supplication, taking care not to overdo
the impression of our distress, which would paralyse
our energies. Therefore, the best of all is a prayer of
absolute confidence in God. God is for our perseverance
more than we are ourselves, it is the success of His work.
He loves and wants our good more than we do ; more
than we do, He cares for our virtue. If we give our will
over to Him, without reserve, He will certainly guard
it from evil.

But a new difficulty crops up. How are we to abandon
our will to Him without ever taking it back again ?
There is only one way for this : to unite ourselves to
the permanent struggle of Jesus Christ against evil ;
to watch with Him.

There is not a single one of our temptations that we
cannot join to our Lord's agony at Gethsemane. In
this gigantic conflict which set Him at grips with all
men's sins, a harrassing conflict that beaded His brow
with blood, our Lord acquired for each of us a strength
capable of overcoming all sollicitations to evil. Jesus
was thrown to the ground, crushed under the weight

of our sins so as to allow all sinners to raise themselves up again victoriously when they had fallen. We have really no excuse for living as if Jesus had not suffered in order to free us from our sins, as if He had not struggled like us, for us, with us, so that we might not enter into temptation.

Let us stop writhing about in temptation like poor birds caught in a snare, alternating " I would like to . . . " with " I cannot ! " At the first approach of temptation let us unite ourselves to Jesus in agony. He will repeat to us the words Pascal heard in his prayer : " *I was thinking of you in my agony, I have spilt so much blood for you* ". Let us unite our hesitations, our difficulties, our anguish, let us unite our virtuous desires also to the holy dispositions of the Saviour. If we watch with Jesus, it is impossible that we should not find the strength to accomplish His divine will, whatever it may be : " *Non mea voluntas sed tua* ".

II.—The temptation from which Jesus redeemed His brethren at Gethsemane is not only that which attacks virtue. He also made Himself, during the deadly hours of His agony, our safeguard in the persecutions we will have to undergo, in all the afflictions which life brings us, in a word, in all our trials.

We must watch against them so that they will not stupefy us in a discouraging sorrow. But how do we fight against feelings, of which we are not masters ? By praying ? But does the blow that strikes us not belie the usefulness of prayer ? If our sorrow knows how to join His suffering, the words of revolt will die on our lips, since He, so much more holy than we, was murdered like one of us. With Him, we will re-discover the candour of childhood which continues to ask for the chalice to be taken away, but, also, the courage of the son who accepts bravely the crucifying will of the

Father. We will offer up with Jesus, behind the darkness of persecution, beyond the mystery of mourning, of sickness, of infirmity, of impoverishing dreams, the necessary expiation for sin and the richness of our suffering for the redemption of our souls, of our families, of our country, of our Church. The Saviour's words to the pilgrims at Emmaus give us the key to all our trials : " Was it not to be expected that the Christ should undergo these sufferings, and enter so into His glory ? " There is no redemption without suffering, but so that our sufferings may redeem us, we must pray with Jesus, watch with Him, and raise ourselves up again with Him.

It may be that events will shortly give us occasion to use this lesson of the Master's. Do not let us see things in a worse light for that would be to make the shadows even darker. Let us keep our outlook far-seeing and lucid. Whatever to-morrow holds for us and whatever worries trouble you above all, fathers of families, about the future of your sons, one certain duty, at least, is on you and on us all, that is, not to give in to discouragement. When he comes near the precipice, the rider does not let the bridle go. Salvation is not in risking everything, like the unfortunate gambler who rushes madly to his ruin. It will not be said that the Catholics of France will fall asleep and will not know how to watch for an hour !

Let us listen, on the contrary, to Christ's victorious instructions. " *Stand firm and watch with me* ". With Him, in all the activity of our prayer and in all that is supernatural in our activity, we will know how to come through the dangerous passes. With Him we will know how to defend the bread, the consciences, the souls of our children. With Him, we will not be afraid to suffer. And if the times we will go through are to make a new social order in history, do not let us forget that by watching and praying with Christ, Catholics are still capable of establishing, in our country, a Christian order.

CHAPTER XVIII

NOT TO FIGHT BUT TO CONQUER ONESELF

Then Simon Peter, who had a sword, drew it, and struck the high priest's servant, cutting off his right ear.

(John XVIII, 10–11. Parallel passages : Matt. XXVI, 51–54 ; Mark. XIV, 47 ; Luke, XXII, 49–51, Cf. 35–38).

JESUS' enemies evidently thought that they would not seize Him without difficulty. Instead of proceeding to arrest Him decisively and quickly, one feels that they hesitated to apprehend Him. Besides, the gang which was helping them was numerous and the high-priest had got a squad of Roman soldiers to assist his own police.

Jesus had just suffered the supreme outrage. Judas, the informer, had kissed Him. The Master released Himself from the sacrilegious embrace of the traitor and faced the crowd. " *Who is it you are looking for ?—Jesus of Nazareth—I am Jesus of Nazareth !* " Then instead of seizing him, these men are suddenly frightened, they fall back and stumble against one another. Getting up quickly, they stay rooted to their places : " *Who is it you are looking for ?* " asked the Saviour—*Jesus of Nazareth —I have told you already that I am Jesus, If I am the man you are looking for, let these others go free* ". And the Master pointed to His disciples.

Meanwhile, for their part, the apostles had reacted differently. Disgusted by Judas' kiss, indignant at the spectacle of this collection of individuals, armed with clubs and cutlasses, encouraged also perhaps by their lack of assurance, they cry : " *Lord shall we strike out with our swords ?* " But Simon Peter did not wait for the reply. He leapt at the officer of the Temple who was at the head of his men ; boldly he aimed at his head, and at the first blow, cut off his right ear.

The attack must have provoked a slight panic among the assailants, of which the Saviour profited to calm the ardour of His Apostle. He did not reprove him ; after all, a case of legitimate defence could be pleaded. He only makes known to him His wish not to have recourse to force. Jesus did not order Peter to get rid of his sword, He only mentioned that it was not the moment to use it. " *Put thy sword back into its place* ' . With a word He repeated the condemnations that He had always pronounced against violence. " *All those who take up the sword will perish by the sword* ". Then He adds, " *But how, were it so, should the Scriptures be fulfilled, which have prophesied that all must be as it is ?* " And alluding to the prayer of His agony, which Peter had not been able to continue with Him : " *Am I not to drink that cup which the Father himself has appointed for me ?* " " *Let them have their way in this* ". He concluded, speaking to His defenders. Then, going to the wounded man (this detail, omitted by the other three evangelists, interested Luke, the doctor), He touched Malchus' ear and healed it.

The high-priest's men had not recovered from their fright or regained their composure, for the Master had time to observe to them that they had taken pointless precautions in coming armed with clubs and swords. Could they not have laid hold of Him when He was teaching every day, seated in the Temple ? At least His disciples were not wrong here ; if He had no need of their swords to defend Him, it was not the power of His adversaries either that put Him at their mercy. It was because He willed it that our Redeemer delivered Himself up to death.

. . . . But His disciples were no longer at His side. They all fled.

Before going over the lesson that our Lord gave His Apostle by the tragic light of torches, we will look at one question which ought to be cleared up first.

Since Jesus was decided not to have recourse to arms how was it that the Apostles were armed? And it appears even more surprising that, according to St. Luke, it seems it could be argued that the Apostles had taken this precaution with the Saviour's formal consent : " *Lord* ", they told Him, " *here are two swords* ", and He said to them, " *That is enough* ".

This passage, in fact, needs some explanation. After having foretold the desertion of His Apostles and Peter's denial, in the Cenacle, St. Luke makes Jesus say : " *Did you go in want of anything, when I sent you out without purse, or wallet, or shoes ?* " *They told Him, nothing !* " *But now is the time* ", He continues, " *for a man to take his purse with him, if he has one, and his wallet too ; and to sell his cloak and buy a sword, if he has none. Believe me, one word has been written that has yet to find its fulfilment in me ; ' and He was counted among the malefactors '. Sure enough all that has been written of Me must be fulfilled* ".

What is the meaning of this warning? Our Lord contrasts two different situations. He recalls first of all the joyous excursions of the Apostles in other times, the missions He had entrusted them with, when the enthusiasms aroused by the Gospel assured them of a cordial and hospitable welcome everywhere. At that time the Master could safely have sent them out without any resources, they would have lacked nothing. That time is over ; from now on, the doors will be closed against them, no one will want to receive them any more. Jesus announced it to them two days before, they will

be persecuted, they will be given up by their kinsmen
and thrown into prison. " All the world will be hating
them because they bear His name " [1]. This is why
they will no longer need to take to the road without
baggage or provisions, because of the ambushes that
will be laid for them, *a sword will be more useful to them
than a cloak*. Let the man who has not got a sword sell
his cloak in order to buy himself one.

It does not seem doubtful that Jesus is using a symbolic
way of speaking here, as He had done already before to
announce to His followers the persecutions that would
be directed against them. " *Do not imagine that I have
come to bring peace to the earth ; I have come to bring a sword,
not peace* " [2]. By a strange paradox, the Gospel which
ought to bring peace on earth, will always arouse men's
hostility here.

But the troubled atmosphere in which the Eucharistic
supper ended, saddened by the departure of the Apostle
who was to be a traitor, had touched the spirit of the
disciples. This word " sword " that Jesus had just
mentioned aggravated their uneasiness, they took everything He said literally. Were there two swords lying
in some corner of the room, or were they the cutlasses
that were used to slaughter the pascal lamb ? " *Lord,
here are two swords . . .* " Jesus knew Himself to be mis-
understood once more and as St. Cyril of Alexandria
supposes, " with an indulgent and rather melancholy
smile ", He contented Himself with replying, " *That
is enough* ". What can be understood by this is ; two
swords are quite enough. Or again, a little ironically ;
that's more than we need. One could also think that
seeing His audience were not grasping what He was
trying to tell them, Jesus simply cut the conversation
short. Now, that's enough !

[1] Luke, XXI, 12–17.
[2] Matt., X, 34.

Whatever explanation one prefers to give to this passage in St. Luke, one could not reasonably find in Jesus' words a call to arms in contradiction with His future attitude. The Saviour knew well that in leaving the Cenacle, He was going to consummate His sacrifice and not to attempt a sudden coup by which He might seize power. If He had had this idea, He will explain to Pilate, " His servants would be fighting to prevent His falling into the hands of the Jews " [1].

A funny battle, for which two poor swords would have been enough ! No, Jesus had no need of His disciple's swords, no more than He would ask for the help of the Angels. Had He not to drink the chalice that His Father had given Him ?

* * * *

We can now weigh, Brethren, the full meaning of the divine teaching to which Peter's gallantry gave rise. Here as everywhere, the circumstances cast light on the Master's thought.

Jesus caught His Apostle's arm and ordered him to put his sword back in its sheath for two reasons. One was His habitual horror of violence. The second was particularly related to the present situation. The mission that Jesus was to accomplish, the religious mission that His disciples and all Christians must carry on absolutely excluded the use of force.

It is worth while noting that on this occasion Our Lord only pronounces directly in the case of religious persecution. He does not cite the principle of legitimate defence, nor the right a citizen might have to resist in circumstances and conditions which are to be determined, grave abuses of powers by a tyrannical or legitimate authority in political, civil or fiscal matters. The Saviour's example cannot be invoked, therefore, to forbid a citizen to revolt against certain unjust laws, or

---

[1] John, XVIII, 36.

against the tyranny of a government whose actions indisputably compromise the common good—to the extent even of the insurrection taking place outside the constitutional means, as long as it does not take on the character of an armed sedition, which latter was always forbidden.

These eventualities, about which the Gospel has inspired Catholic morality with precise rules, are in a different domain from the situation in which Jesus finds Himself at Gethsemane. All the same, we should realise that they do not escape the general rule formulated by the Master " *All those who take up the sword will perish by the sword* ". Except in the case of legitimate defence, that is to say, when one's life is attacked and one can only save it by using force, except in that case, the Christian is not authorised to take to the sword. Violence is, in itself, immoral. The whole Gospel proclaims it. The pronouncement at Gethsemane insists moreover on its results ; violence is useless, it is harmful.

A conflict which can be settled when the adverse parties stick loyally to the right and the just will never be solved by violence. The man who yields momentarily to force will seek for the opportunity of revenge. On the other hand, the most powerful person who has been able to impose his will by arms on a weaker adversary will come across, some day, someone more powerful still who will in his turn put him down. History, alas ! gives abundant illustrations of these mysterious laws of an imminent justice.

But once we enter into strictly religious terrain, the very idea of violence ought to be put to one side, even if it is to be exercised in the name of legitimate defence ; not only because violence as always brings in its train sad reprisals, but because it is in formal contradiction with the spirit of charity and of peace, which are the very characteristics of religion.

Is this to mean that a persecuted Christian ought not defend himself? He ought! We ought to defend the rights of the Christian conscience, especially when they are violated to the detriment of the powerless children, or the poor. We ought to defend the spiritual rights of the Church, with courageous firmness, but without departing from the spirit of the Gospel. The Saviour sent us " *like sheep among wolves* ". We should betray His cause if we adopted the methods of the wolves.

At the beginning of this century Pope Pius X in his Encyclical *Gravissimo* recommended the persecuted Catholics of France " to fight for the Church with perseverance and energy, without acting, at the same time, in a seditious or violent manner. It was not by " violence ", maintained the Pope, " but by firmness and constancy that they would come to break the obstinacy of their enemies ". The Sovereign Pontiff's orders were a faithful echo of the Saviour's command.

Certainly, Brethren, when we are confronted with an adversary who despises the most elementary justice and does not hesitate to use trickery and lies, our instinctive gesture is not patience, but indignation, and counter-attack. We would get some consolation in tweaking his ear, if we had not gone as far as cutting one off for him, as St. Peter did! Is it not excusable to oppose with force men who abuse the strength they are given? Excusable, perhaps ; legitimate, not at all!

Jesus, doubtless, excused Peter's first thoughtless action, but He did not allow him to continue. " *Put thy sword back into its sheath* ".

The Kingdom of God does not assert itself by violence ; religion is not implanted by force. Between the avenging sword and the chalice of His sufferings, Jesus chooses the sword. He triumphed not by the sword, but by His sacrifice, by His death. Following His example, the Church ought to put up with violence, but never exercise it at all herself, and she will carry off her most resounding victories thanks to the sufferings of her children and the blood of her martyrs. Now, this is not a doctrine of passivity, but on the contrary a call to energy and coolness which, when put to the service of truth, will be infinitely more fruitful than the use of force.

" I send you forth like lambs among wolves ". Jesus is not afraid to leave us unarmed before the wolves, He is not afraid of the ferocity of the wolves for our sake. What He is worried about, in relation to us, is the wolf in sheep's clothing, the adversary who houses us, flatters us, lulls to sleep, or the traitor who kisses us. Jesus fears, for His Church's sake, the favours of power and the dangers of well-being, much more than persecutions. On the contrary He knows she is safe when she lacks human security.

The sword He threw to the ground ; the only one with which He arms us is the one whose edge will cut away our egoistic nature. The true Christian is not someone who stirs up trouble, but he is a fighter.

The Master never even thought of fighting the brigands who had come to arrest Him ! What good would that have done ? And if they were successful, what would it have proved ? He had just undergone another struggle, costly in a different way, kneeling on the rock of His Agony, and He had triumphed in it by accepting the chalice of His Father's rigorous wishes.

So, Brethren, we ought to fight with Jesus Christ and for Jesus Christ, but not with swords against people armed with clubs. We will fight fiercely first of all against our evil inclinations, then against error, against sin, against the perversity of customs, against the injustice of tyrants, by observing all God's wishes strictly and patiently ; by loving, living, dying in a holy manner.

CHAPTER XIX

JESUS CANNOT BE FOLLOWED AT A DISTANCE

*And those who had arrested Jesus led him away into
the presence of the high-priest, Caiphas, where the
scribes and elders had assembled. Yet Peter
followed him at a long distance, as far as the high-
priest's palace.*

(Matt. XXVI, 57–58).

IT is necessary for us, Brethren, to make an effort to
realise the collapse of the Apostles caused by Jesus'
arrest. All that we could imagine it to be would probably
be less than the reality.

It is easy to put their flight down to fear. Jesus'
anticipatory judgment on them was less summary. In
warning them of the trials which they would undergo
that night, He had used the best word to cover it,
" scandal ".

This, in fact, was the cause of their confusion. Although
Jesus had warned them of it on numerous occasions,
without hiding a single detail from them, they could
not accept the idea that their Master, in whom they
recognised the Messiah, who had named Himself as
the Son of God before their very eyes, should have to
experience a defeat, and such a total one at that, and
in such humiliating circumstances.

Let us put ourselves in their place : in the twinkling
of an eye, they see the hope that they have entertained
for two years, day after day, vanishing. Apparently
they were fooled ! All that they have sacrificed for
Jesus has been pure loss. The personal loss that they

167

feel is nothing to the catastrophe in which their faith is engulfed. Let us try to understand the distress, into which the avowal they have, in their confusion, just made plunges them. " So it wasn't true . . . ! " It was the Pharisees who were right to deny Jesus the title of Messiah. He was not the One for whom Israel was waiting ; it was not He who would found the kingdom of God !

They certainly do not think that their Master, who is so humble, so good, so holy, could have deliberately led them into error ; Jesus did not want to fool them, He was fooled Himself. God obviously disowned Him, since He abandoned Him to the hands of His enemies. Could the apostles' faith resist such sorrowful evidence ? . . .

So it would be harsh to refuse to accept any excuse for their precipitate flight. But Simon Peter's conduct will only be esteemed more, for he, disconcerted at first like the others, got a grip on himself later and came back.

The fourth Gospel gives him a companion, " *Simon Peter followed Jesus* ", we read " *with another disciple* " [1] For many commentators, this other disciple might be St. John himself, but another very old tradition identifies him with John Mark, who, belonging to a well-known family in Jerusalem, could be " acquainted with the high-priest " more reasonably than the son of Zebedee, and could facilitate Peter's entry into the court. Peter could have met him besides just outside the palace, which would make St. John's narrative agree with St. Matthew's and St. Mark's ; these latter limited themselves to writing, " *Yet Peter followed him at a long distance as far as the high-priest's palace* ".

But here we find ourselves, Brethren, faced with very mysterious things. Simon Peter began by fleeing with the other Apostles ; suddenly he stops. His affection for the Saviour wins over all his other feelings. He does

---

[1] John, XVIII, 15.

not ask himself whether he is going to commit a new imprudence ; the others, actually, are only conforming to Jesus' desire, Who had asked the soldiers to let the disciples go free. But he only listens to his heart, he cannot abandon his Master like that, he must know the fate that awaits Him. He comes back down the road, he sees the flickering red light of the torches through the olive trees, and he follows the escort that is taking Jesus away.

There is no doubt about it : in this place Peter shows himself to be the most loving and bravest of all the Apostles. And this is what will bring about his fall. If he had stayed with the others, the occasion would not have arisen for him to disown his Master ; but because he loves Him more than the others do, because he cannot be separated from Him, he is walking towards the high-priest's dwelling, where, three times, he will be ashamed of the Jesus for Whom he had been ready to die ! He would not have sinned if he had loved less ! . . . .

Aren't the arrangements of Providence obscure ? However, can we not suppose (I will use the word that comes instinctively to our lips, the word, which is brought out as an excuse by so many sinners) that the " fatality " which made Peter fall contained, in the intentions of Providence, a beneficial instruction for us who offend God at the same time as we love Him ? Theoretically, the two terms are contradictory. Our heart cannot love Him and drive Him away at the same time. But in fact (and in stating it we are sincere) we disobey Him, although we sincerely do not stop loving Him. This is not possible, nevertheless it is. Whoever is able can solve this contradiction. At least, Peter's example reassures us about our own wickedness, which is less profound perhaps than it seems, since Peter who loved Jesus so much more than us, succumbed like us.

Very often too, it is in wanting to do good, to do more

than our duty, to do better than others, that we have been guilty of imprudence, or awkwardness that ended in sin. The wise men, who stay far from danger, condemn our rashness in the name of the principle that " the better is often the enemy of the good ". God, Who reads hearts, will be more indulgent perhaps to our too impulsive nature, for while Peter, when he is bombarded with questions, is losing his head and swearing that he does not know Him, Jesus Himself knows well that even then Peter loves Him more than the others do.

*　　*　　*　　*

The short sentence in St. Matthew on which we are meditating contains four words which have earned the Apostle Peter severe criticism, " *Yet Peter followed him at a long distance . . .* " Those who enjoy the easy sport of remaking history after the event do not forgive him this remoteness. But, good people, we would like to know how you would have behaved in his place !

The high-priest's police had not forgotten his brusque attack at the time of the arrest, how would they look on his approaching the Saviour again ? On recognising him, they would immediately have suspected him of wanting to rescue their victim, and for fear of a new attack they would have caught him and tied him up, and then condemned the disciple at the same time as the Master. That was all that Peter asked for : To die with Jesus ! It was our Lord (we saw why) who said to him, " *I am going where thou canst not follow me now* ". Peter must not die at this time, and he would be going to his death if, after the incident with the sword, he were to take his place beside Jesus.

Yet in spite of everything the course of events does not give the lie to those who blame Simon Peter's denial on his following of Jesus at a distance. Not having gone into the High-priest's court with the crowd, he had to parley to get the gate open, and it is just because he followed Jesus from too great a distance that he came to tell the first lie which he could not afterwards retract.

A Benedictine commentator of the IXth Century wrote quite rightly : " Peter could not have denied the Saviour if he had stayed by His side ". The ancient writer does not say " if he had *come back* ", but, " if he had *stayed* by His side." This time we understand. Indeed, Peter could have stayed by Jesus' side, if he had not drawn his sword without orders to do so and, above all, if he had known how to watch and pray with the Saviour. He could then have accompanied Him to the end, confining himself to suffering in silence.

Peter, who might have stayed, could no longer return to Jesus' side, and that is the tragedy of his misadventure. Having abandoned Him in the beginning he could only follow Jesus afterwards *at a long distance*. At a distance, now quickening his step so as not to lose sight of them, now slowing up so as not to attract attention, all the time waiting for an opportune moment to rejoin Him. But however short the distance that separated him from his Master, that gap was still too great ; between Jesus and Peter, who was following Him at a distance, there was unluckily room for three poor little temptations. And Jesus died without Peter rejoining Him . . . .

* * * *

We need do no more than change a pronoun, Brethren, in the Gospel's short sentence, in order to pick out the cause of our own failings, slight faults or grave faults, passing relapses or long periods of luke-warmness. *Sequebatur eum a longe :* we followed Him at a long distance.

Sometimes we are impatient as we note the slowness

of the progress of the kingdom of God on earth, and some people, with a rare injustice, blame Providence for this. We should rather contrast the tiny number of Christians who follow Jesus closely, with the great majority of the baptised. Among these latter, how many are there not who are the equivalent of apostates? Above them there are the people who believe they are being nice to us in declaring that they are not hostile to religion. Pilate did not have any animosity towards Jesus either. Add up all the categories of fine folk, who are not actually such very fine folk, the people who are afraid to compromise themselves, the people who disguise their convictions in circles where Christ is suspect, controversial, embarrassing. Catholics for whom religion is a world label, the stamp of guarantee on their social privileges, the intermittent disciples who recognise Christ publicly on Sunday morning and who for the rest of the week "know not the man".

If one observes just how these nominal adherents of Christianity make up the majority of the baptised, then instead of doubting the fruitfulness of the Gospel, won't one be even more astonished at the supernatural power of the Church, which is capable of continuing her sanctifying mission to the world, in spite of the enormous dead weight she is obliged to drag with her? Mankind follows Christ with a disheartening slowness, because there are too many Christians who only follow Jesus at a distance, at a very great distance.

Would to Heaven we had never had to address this reproach to ourselves! Blessed are those who can bear witness that they have never turned their backs on Jesus Christ. But still who has ever regularly followed Him closely?

He is followed certainly, and in order to follow Him we must make renunciations and give proofs of our courage. But Jesus is always advancing and He walks quickly, Nature needs rest, relaxation. One stops for a breath and when one sets out again Jesus is a little further off, He has not been lost sight of, He is still followed, but contact with Him has been lost, His grace slips away from us, and our ardour cools again.

Christians we certainly are, and at the difficult corners we run for a while to catch up with Him. But our Lord wants us to be Christians every hour of the day, in all the details of our existance, in our business and in the street, at work and in our leisure hours, towards others as much as for ourselves. One is never finished being a Christian ! Sometimes one must speak and sometimes be silent, one must push oneself forward when one would prefer to rest quietly, then efface oneself when one feels like showing oneself off. One must watch oneself and forget oneself by turns, quicken one's pace and slow it up, save one's energy and go all out in devotion, deprive oneself and give oneself, suffer and smile . . . . How could one not show signs of fatigue very quickly? Like children coming back from a walk, one drags one's legs and loses ground little by little ; Let's take a breath, let's live just like everybody else without superfluous obsessions, then we will rejoin Jesus in a minute . . .

In that minute we will have met temptation perhaps ; perhaps we will deny Him in that minute !

* * * *

Let us profit, Brethren, from Simon Peter's unfortunate experience, when one goes away from our Lord, one often only finds Him again by taking the road of repentance, that is to say, after having sinned. And we have good reason to come back as quickly as possible, and with absolute confidence in His mercy, but it would be so much better *to remain* always *by His side*. And, taking all in all, so much easier.

Only two things are needed to commit a sin : *negligence* and an *occasion of sin*. The occasion of sin can always surprise us, it does not depend on ourselves, but it is up to us whether we give in to negligence or avoid it. Now, to follow Jesus from a distance is to neglect Him.

Negligentia is the opposite of *diligentia*. In one we find care, exactitude, zeal. In the other carelessness, forgetfulness, coolness. *Diligere* means to love someone chosen from a thousand others, *Neglegere* means not to pay attention, to have no preferences, to be detached. Negligence is a lack of attention (in the singular) and a want of attentions (in the plural) and both take us away from Jesus.

Lack of attention which can extend from simple illusion to blindness. If Peter had observed himself more he would have spotted the moment when his first impulse of beautiful generosity veered towards imprudence and rashness. Let us be attentive therefore to the first warnings of our conscience and severe in correcting the first deviations of our imagination or our sensibility. From the moment that we feel ourselves drawn by a natural inclination, let us oppose our strongest desires for goodness to the call from below. Before acting let us raise our *looks* towards Jesus. But also let us surround Him with *attentions*.

Peter's great mistake was not to watch with Jesus, not to keep his thoughts and his will constantly united to those of his Master. Our will, in fact, would not be separated from Jesus' if we turn a loving thought towards Him frequently. Let us get used to seeking out and savouring His presence, first of all, in the regular exercise of prayer ; that is where He is waiting for us and where He makes Himself heard. Then in the exercise of charity, it is in the persons of our brethren and especially the least of them that He loves to be served as He uses them to make Himself loved.

Don't let us disdain the little prayers or the little duties, the little virtues or the little sacrifices. The man who shows himself to be faithful in little things is the good servant who follows Jesus closely. Let us do nothing by halves for Him Who did not love us by halves. " I did not love you for amusement . . . " He said to St. Angela. He has a right to a total gift of ourselves.

His very intransigence is a sign of His love for us. If He wants us by His side it is to persuade us in the end to walk with His step. By His side we are safe. The man who follows Jesus at a distance finds neither peace nor happiness in religion. Joy is for the brave people who go to meet suffering, for those who are not afraid to follow Jesus from close at hand when men desert Him.

This time again and more than ever, let us end our meditation less with a resolution than with a prayer. We run so many risks of going away from Him, that to prevent ourselves from yielding to them, it is vital that the Saviour should hold us by the hand. Let us repeat frequently the supplication that comes before our Holy Communion, " *A te nunquam seperari permittas*. Never allow me, Lord, to be parted from Thee ".

CHAPTER XX

FROM IMPRUDENCE TO DENIAL.

I do not know the man you speak of.
(Mark XIV, 71).

IN the sermon which he gave in the Louvre on our Lord's Passion, Bossuet, reviewing the sorrows that Jesus endured and remarking on the pain that Simon Peter's downfall caused Him, expressed himself in this manner about the disciple : " How firm he is ! How intrepid ! He wants to die for his Master, he cannot leave Him. He follows Him in the beginning but, Oh the faithfulness that he started out with and that only served to pierce Jesus' heart with a crueller denial, a more criminal perfidy " [1]. May Bossuet forgive me if " the perfidy of St. Peter " strikes me as less evident than the treacheries of an eloquence that is capable of leading the greatest orators astray.

Peter, treacherous ! Peter, disloyal ! Peter, cruel ! On what might one claim to base these judgments ? I read and re-read the Gospel and I only succeed in finding there a poor, dreadfully unfortunate Peter. For the rest, if our sacred books have reported all the details of his fault for us, it is only for our instruction. Let us try to understand it well rather than dismiss the man who gives it to us.

" Peter went into the high-priest's court ", writes St. Matthew, " *to see the end* ". One can interpret this expression in an optimistic sense, and see the Apostle, in spite of everything, still hoping that things will settle

---

[1] *Carême du Louvre*, Good Friday, 7th April, 1662.

themselves yet. It can mean, on the contrary, that Peter, having lost confidence, thought that all was finished and this discouragement would also partially excuse his failings. But, whatever the Apostle's private thoughts were, whether he believed in his Master's safety or ruin, one cannot deny him two equally admirable sentiments ; an indefectible love for Jesus (whether He is condemned or released, Peter will be near Him, he wants to throw in his lot with the Saviour's), then a rare courage which makes him despise danger. In going, alone of all the disciples, into the haunt of his enemies, he is not unaware of the risk he is running of being arrested in his turn. He has not changed, he is always ready to die with Jesus.

No, he has not changed when he penetrates into the palace court. However, in an hour's time, he will have changed completely, to the point of being unrecognizable. He will tremble before sarcasms, he will disown the dearest friend of his life . . .

Such is the terrible lesson that we must meditate, Brethren ; this change which is as quick as it is unreasonable—the terrible surprise of the temptation that roughly overthrows the strongest—the desolating weakness of our ever vulnerable nature—in all, our deepseated insecurity in regard to evil which lays us low before we can defend ourselves. That is the true *perfidy*, but it is the treachery of sin which, in a few seconds, can change a Christian into a sceptical mocker, a dissenting rebel, a dishonest businessman, a jealous brother, an unfaithful husband.

Between sunset and dawn a man can burn what he adored, stop praying and believing, negative a laboriously acquired capital of honour and virtue because he will have fallen unexpectedly into sin, the sin he was not watching out for, the sin he thought himself incapable of. This sin will have upset his whole life, turned his

convictions upside down, changed his affections and
made him another man.

The surprise of the sin appeared in the very facility
with which it was committed. That is all it is, a sin ;
the time needed to say *Yes* when one thought *No,* or
vice versa.

His conscience scarcely struggled, the sinner felt
himself slipping into a gulf. He cannot even, most
times, plead the violence of the temptation in his defence.
How many times before he had thwarted just as pressing
solicitations quite victoriously ! When the evil desires
are most ardent, one might say that they provoke a
more energetic reaction in us, and it is often a slight
temptation that brings about the grave fault, but also
a temptation, to which it seems the sinful will had
already given a tacit consent. Thus, without one having
the time to oppose it, the sin that was ignored up till
then, the reputedly impossible sin, became the accomplished sin, the sin with which one does not know
where one is any more. Could I have done that ?
When we think of the circumstances of our past faults
we cannot cite a single sin that we might not have
avoided.

Simon Peter was the victim of this *unexpectedness of
sin,* he was conquered by the unforeseen force of little
temptations. For neither had he, on the night of his
fault, to put up with very formidable temptations. The
tempters, at least, were not much of a crowd, the door-
keeper, servants, valets. Peter had withstood rougher
attacks than those that gave rise to his denials. For
years now he had seen the élite of his fellow-countrymen
cutting themselves off from Jesus, the most virtuous of
all, the Pharisees, the most learned, the Scribes, the
most religious, the priests. He had seen longstanding
disciples of Jesus leaving Him en masse at Capharnaum,
and instead of this departure shaking his faith, it made

him more attached to the Lord. What weight could the mockery or the curiosity of the high-priest's household have beside the sacrifices he had known? He had given up his trade, his house, his family! He, a coward? Did he hesitate to compromise himself shortly before in the garden? He fought for the good and did not miss his mark. He, a liar? The man who does not know how to sham, the character that is all of a piece! . . . .

And suddenly, Peter is going to lose his assurance, he is going to waver and to lie not before those enemies of the Lord, who from now on are to be all-powerful, (they are in the interior of the palace) but before the mercenaries, ignorant and indifferent people. How can one explain such a sudden change?

* * * *

But, Brethren, this suddenness is really only an illusion. Nature does not proceed by dramatic leaps. A sudden death is the foreseeable result of a slow wearing down of the organism, or sudden bankruptcy is the inevitable conclusion of a series of irregular operations. The wall that collapses suddenly had been undermined for a long time. In the same way the sudden fall of a soul into sin is only sudden in appearance. It is, in reality, the fruit of some previous obscure operation.

The time that a Christian succumbs to temptation is rarely when he is most guilty, however grave his fault may be in itself or its consequences either. He was much more guilty before his sin, when he was playing with fire, when, pushing the thought of sin weakly away from him, he familiarised himself with it, for during that time the desires of pride asserted themselves, the appetites of the senses became more imperious, or the calls of interest turned around his obsession. All that was needed then was the opportunity (which itself is unforeseeable), for him suddenly to deny his dignity, his promises, his faith.

The suddenness of sin is only apparent. A sin is begun long before it is actually committed. When our Lord announced Peter's denial to him, He was only foretelling the sudden " circumstance " in which His Apostle would give way, but Peter had been carrying the true cause of his downfall within himself for some time.

Before one can rely on a rope, a chain, a dike or a fortres , one must be sure, in every case, that there is no weak point where, when traction or pressure are brought to bear on it, the inevitable rupture will not take place. It is the same with a soul's resistance, our most certain virtues, our most solid qualities are insufficient guarantees of strength, if we have not picked out *our weak spot* from them, the one that must be constantly protected, watched, propped up.

Peter possessed immense qualities, otherwise would the Master have had such a marked predilection for him, and would He have chosen him as the head of His Church ? However Peter had a weak point, one alone, but one we have met regularly in all the situations where the Gospel introduces him, and this was his impulsiveness. In spite of the harm it caused him, and although Jesus had taken him up so many times on this subject, Peter did not want to account for it even when Jesus openly condemned the presumptuous impulses to which it was leading him. In vain Jesus urged him to watch, and to pray too, so as to forearm himself against the dangers he would have to face, Peter was a man of the moment. He owed his ever ardent generosity, no doubt, his frankness, his lack of self-interest, his courage to his impulsive nature. There is not the slightest element of calculation in him, he is a man for the first impulse. But his impulsiveness is also his weakness, for he does not calculate either when it is needed. Impressionable, he acts without reflecting, and having made a mistake, he falls from one imprudence into another, he harms himself, he loses his powers, he succumbs.

And we are all there with him. Temptation always attacks our weak point, and if we do not defend this weak point, temptation infallibly lays us low, in spite of all there is in us of good and sometimes sanctity. If the weak point yields, sin unfolds itself in remorseless succession against which we are henceforward powerless, because we made ourselves powerless.

* * * *

What happened to our dear unfortunate Simon Peter was good. If we do not lose sight of the fact that impulsiveness is the weak point in his nature, we can go over the circumstances of his fall in our spirit without giving vent to scandalised cries, for we see with what frightening ease a soul, otherwise virtuous, hurls itself into grave sin.

The door-keeper, rightly distrusting all strangers, especially on a night of such commotion, eyes him with a suspicious glare. What brought this stranger here at such an hour? Why does he want to come in? Without doubt, he is one of the disciples of that man they have just arrested. She asks him if he is, it is only natural. Naturally also, Peter having only one objective, to get into the place, brushes his questioner aside, " Me? No ! "

He said that without reflecting. Do his good intentions not excuse a white lie " which does no harm to anyone ", according to the sacred phrase? (A lie always harms the person who tells it.) The Apostle's first impulse, his reflex, could have been completely different. Peter could have looked the door-keeper coolly in the eye and said " Yes ". She would probably have limited herself to advising him not to make a scene. He said " No ", without reflecting, so as not to have to give lengthy explanations, because it was simpler. But he was about to experience that psychological law, which binds us to our actions, " masters of our first action, we are slaves of our second ". So now he is the prisoner of his first action, of his little white lie.

Once in the court, he cannot just stand still. He heads for the braisier around which the servants are warming themselves. In the darkness, he would have passed unnoticed, but the flame lights up his face, heads turn towards this man who does not belong to the house and seems to be very upset. There is no harm meant by the reflection addressed to him, " *Thou too wast with Jesus the Nazarene* ".

Peter has just said " no ", can he go back on it ? And once more, what he says does not commit anyone : " *Woman, I do not understand what thou meanest !* " He has said neither yes, nor no. He still keeps his *incognito*. But another law is coming into play against him. Jesus had often repeated it ; concerning His person, neutrality is impossible. " Whosoever is not with me is against me ! " To put oneself above the uproar is a way of deserting. In wishing to be nothing more than a spectator Peter leaves the ranks of Jesus' friends and defenders. One cannot be a spectator with regard to Christianity, one must choose : to be for Christ, or against Him. There is no intermediary position. The unfortunate Apostle is going to find this out.

He quickly realised that this was not the proper company for him, on the other hand, he does not want to go away, and how could he retreat ? To save his face, he stretches his hands out to the fire, as if his only worry is to warm himself. How cold he must have been, poor Peter ! The crowd there talk about the events of the day, from time to time a guard or a maid-servant comes out to keep them up to date with what is going on inside. Things are going badly with Jesus ! Peter is being tortured. His glance slips stealthily towards the room where his Master is being interrogated. For the full hour he is there, he must keep up his share of the conversation, or else he will arouse suspicion. He says his say, as briefly as possible. Perhaps he would like to know what replies the accused is making to the grievances alleged against Him. Peter shows a little too much interest in what is taking place. Peter talks too much, his accent gives him away. " *But thou art Galilean* " the crowd cry out, " *thou canst not deny it. Thou art of that band* ". If he is, the next man improves on it, " *I recognise thee, I saw thee in the garden with Him !* "

Peter feels himself closed in on all sides, then he is distracted, he does not know what he is saying, he is out of his depth, he staggers under the accusations and then he blurts out, " *I swear to you !* " and as if this were not enough, he starts swearing " May heaven strike me if I am not telling the truth ! " " *I do not know the man you speak of* ".

He did not however mention Jesus by name, " I do not know *the man* you speak of ! " At that very moment the cock is heard crowing. Peter remembers Jesus' prophesy immediately. He gets up and goes off, followed by the sneers of the guards and servants. He finishes where he should have begun. His lies did not convince anyone. They just served to bring about his shame and his remorse. He sinned like a fool, he sinned for nothing ! If a finger gets caught in the gear-mechanism, the whole arm will be dragged in.

There are no half measures with sin. Once one is on the way down, one cannot climb back, one can do nothing more, one does not want to do anything more, one does not know what one is doing any more. There is no way of holding back, the fall is inevitable. And how quickly one finds one has fallen, fallen very low, without malice, without revolt, stupidly, through weakness, for two or three imprudences.

Peter denied his Master ! but was it not rather himself he denied ? In a moment of madness, he disowned his upright life, his vocation, his promises, the hope that God had in him. His past, his future, his whole life, collapses . . . . . .

* * * *

Dearly beloved Brethren, we are not more solid than poor Simon, whom divine grace wanted to make, and, nonetheless, could make into a " rock ". May his downfall enlighten us, at least !

There is an expressive phrase that is sometimes used, when people say about a sinner that he " *gives way to evil* ", and that is just what he does, he gives way to sin, he surrenders without fighting, he capitulates, abdicates. As long as he struggles, with God's help, he can conquer evil desires. A person only sins because he does not fight, because he puts himself out of action. Also it is not at the moment that temptation is unloosed on one, that one must run to arms ; then, it is often too late. A passion of which one is no longer master has become one's master instead. We must discipline our passions, safeguard ourselves against wicked influences from outside, and forbid ourselves the *least imprudences* while there is still time and while danger is far off.

In our last meditation we observed at what point simple negligences are fatal. How ought one not judge imprudences ? Some people try to excuse themselves —or reassure themselves—by saying : It is not a sin, only an indiscretion. Only ? Maybe this is graver. Let us understand this. In strict doctrine, an indiscretion is not yet a sin, at any rate, a grave sin. But that is where the danger lies. Coming point-blank face to face with certain sin, the Christian who was still on guard would experience horror, he would not commit it, he would right himself immediately. The danger of imprudences is that they fool us. Little by little they put our vigilance to sleep, they dull the edge of our conscience, they lessen the repugnance that sin aroused in us at the beginning, they make us see the law and the divine demands as less strict than they are ; they make in conjunction the scope of the liberties we allow ourselves even greater. In parallel fashion, as one borders on sin without succumbing to it, one presumes about one's own strength. One day, sin will no longer frighten us, and then we are disarmed and we fall. This is the inevitable result of indiscretions.

Peter remembered Jesus' words. He recalls his vain protestations of courage. " *Though all else should lose courage over thee, I will never lose mine!*" Not I! These are the words he used to the servants in Caiphas' house, " *Thou art one of his disciples ?—Not I !* "

Let us be prudent and above all let us be humble, all of us, even the best of us, even those with fifty years of virtue behind them. As long as we fear sin, as long as we believe that we can commit it, our faithfulness is safe. Let us rather turn St. Peter's words around, " When all will be sure of never sinning, I won't be sure ! "

CHAPTER XXI

REPENTANCE AND PARDON

*And the Lord turned, and looked at Peter ; and
Peter remembered what the Lord had said to him . . . .
And Peter went out, and wept bitterly.*

(Luke XXII, 61–62).

IF it does not take long to clear the distance that separates
the state of grace from that of sin, less time still is needed
for a sinner to become a saint. Peter took an hour to
fall ; but in an instant he rights himself and sets about
raising himself higher than he was before his fall.

As we have done with the circumstances of his error,
so we will consider his repentance, not forgetting that
God wanted to turn the momentary weakness of the
Apostle not to his own good only, but to ours as well.

*   *   *   *

" *Then came the second cock-crow* . . . " St. Mark is
the only one of the Evangelists to mention two crowings
of the cock. His position as St. Peter's disciple confers
a particular authority to this passage of his narrative.
We are therefore justified in believing that a first warning
cry rang out, before the one that brought the guilty
man to his senses ; doubtless, in his upset state, he had
not paid attention to it, afterwards, recalling the stages
of his falling away, he realised that he had neglected
the supreme warning of grace.

In fact, Brethren, God never withdraws himself from
the sinner. God, Who catches him up when he succumbs,
also warns him from the beginning of his temptation !

But this preliminary intervention of grace often passes unnoticed. The sinner only hears the first crowing of the cock confusedly. As an excuse for his fault he alleges that he found himself all alone when he had to battle with the seductions and the desires of sin. At that moment, it is true, no other thought occupied his mind. His previous resolutions? Gone! The idea of duty? Forgotten! He thinks of neither the urgency of the divine law to himself, nor the fear of eternal sanctions nor the threat of the immediate consequences of his fault : that is, his own bitterness and affliction or the sorrow of his people. Nothing matters now but his passion, his interest, his pleasure. He was alone! Afterwards he says " My God, why were you so far away from me while I was being tempted? "

Do not let us believe that God can remain the unmoved and silent witness of our moral struggles. There would be no " temptation " if there were no debate of conscience, and conscience does not stay silent of its own accord. But if we are slow in obeying it, the appeals of passion quickly make it recover its voice and stifle our better impulses completely. When the thought of God, or of good or of duty has disappeared, then one has already " entered into temptation ", one has given a first consent to it, the sin has begun.

Once it is completely committed, the advantages it bore with it give way to the shame of having obtained it at the price of a capitulation. Disillusionment and sadness follow a tasted pleasure almost instantaneously. Appeased passion is set slumbering again, conscience tears off its gag. Deaf to its stifled appeal when it first gave the alarm, the sinner now hears its voice distinctly, but now it is the voice of the Judge condemning him. " *Then came the second cock-crow ; and Peter remembered* . . .

* * * *

He had refused to believe in the danger, when his Master was warning him of it: " Thou shalt disown me thrice ! " He had objected to the insult of such a suspicion. And this was the man who has just said " *I know nothing of the man !* " He was ashamed of the Master who had given evidence of greater friendship for him than for the others. Jesus had performed one of His first miraculous healings for him, He had made him to walk on the waves, He had revealed His glory to him on Thabor. By way of thanks to the immense goodness of the Saviour, he had just denied all knowledge of Him, he, Cephas, the head of the Apostles and the man who should have been their model ! What was the point of his getting worked up against Judas ? He had degraded himself to the level of the traitor. Would it not have been better for him also never to have been born ? Why did he not get himself killed immediately in the garden ? If he could only die now . . . . . ! Peter is crushed by the shame of his fault.

But shame can only burden the sinner, weigh him down, it will never raise him up again. Although sorrow for having caused our brethren pain is allied sometimes to shame or even the supernatural desolation of having offended God, it usually only means personal suffering. One despises oneself for having been wicked or cowardly, or vile ; one is angry at oneself for having fallen beneath one's level and the level of others. And this vexation, this humiliation are the true reactions of a wholly human dignity. There is nothing here that is beyond the order of nature. Our nature is weak and we sin, our nature is honest and we blush for having sinned. As for remorse, far from lessening our responsibility, it only makes it more intolerable. Our disgust, our disavowals, our regrets have no power to give us peace.

To what despairing solutions might St. Peter not have abandoned himself, if the Saviour had not snatched him from his shame, in order to inspire him with a holy repentance ? Do not let us confuse one with the other, shame paralyses, repentance gives courage. Shame is a confusion of self-love, repentance is an act of humility which favours generous reparations.

While the unfortunate Peter was piling denial on denial, Caiphas, having finished interrogating Jesus, but being obliged in the meantime to wait for day-break in order to convoke the Sanhedrin, had his prisoner taken to the dungeons. The guards who had been teasing Simon Peter, left him and went, tittering, to fulfil the high-priest's orders, and Jesus came out of the audience chamber at the very moment that the cock's crowing was ringing out. Then, writes St. Luke, " *the Lord turned and looked at Peter* " . . .

These four words of the Gospel are of the kind that one's spirit cannot contemplate for long without one wanting to fall on one's knees. Peter, crushed by the unworthiness of his conduct, sees the escort that is leading his Master away, and Jesus, indifferent to the injuries of his accusers and the brutality of the servants who jostle and cuff him, turns towards the guilty Apostle. *Conversus Dominus, respexit Petrum.*

Their looks meet. Peter would like to bow his head, but he cannot tear his eyes from Him, Whom he has just denied. He knows the Saviour's looks well ; that look that had determined his vocation, he had not been able to resist either its authority or its charm ; and that tender look of the Master's on the day He had affirmed, looking at His disciples, " Here are my brethren, my sisters, my mother ! " And that look that had made him tremble when, he, Simon, had wanted to banish the Cross from Jesus' path ! And the affectionately pitying look with which he had invited the too-rich young man to follow him ! And His look, clouded with tears, before Lazarus' tomb . . . He knows them well.

the Saviour's looks. And yet never, never had he seen on the Saviour's face the expression he sees there at this moment, the eyes marked with sadness but without any severity. A look of reproach, without a doubt, but which becomes suppliant at the same time and seems to repeat to him " *Simon, I have prayed for thee !* "

This look only rests on him for an instant, Jesus was violently dragged away by the soldiers, but Peter sees Him all the time. He sees the Saviour's indulgent look not weighing up but alighting on the smarting wound of his fault. This look increases his remorse and at the same time chases the horrible temptations of dispair from his heart. Peter hears the Saviour's voice within him " I told you so, my Peter . . . . . I, I always know you, you will never be disowned by me ! Don't get discouraged, Peter. Remember the story of the Good Shepherd who is so happy to bring back on his shoulders the sheep that strayed—remember the story that shocked you so much, the father throwing himself about the neck of the son, who after leaving him, dishonoured him, and then came back confident and trembling to ask his forgiveness ; remember the Good Samaritan, and Mary Magdalene, and Zacheus . . . . Did I not say it to you often enough, that I have not come to call the just but the sinners ? . . . Peter, don't be hesitant any longer ! By doubting your pardon you would deny me most atrociously and this time perhaps finally ! "

And Peter remembered everything Jesus had said . . .

What sinner, Brethren, if he turns with faith towards our Saviour, can grow hardened in his fault ? And what guilty person who is repentant can doubt the divine mercy ? One of the most beautiful hymns of the Breviary, composed by St. Ambrose, invites us to beg Christ for this gentle look which merited forgiveness for us.

Jesu, labantes respice,
Et nos videndo corrige.

"Jesus, look at us when we are succumbing, for thy look sets us right".

Si respicis, labes cadunt
Fletuque culpa solvitur !

"When thou lookest at us, our stains disappear, falling away like scales, and the tears that thy eyes cause to spring from ours, cleanse us of our faults".

* * * *

And Peter went out, and wept bitterly. The Apostle can obviously no longer stay in the high-priest's house, his sobs would point him out too clearly to the malice of the servants, and the latter would turn on him in derision after his perjury. That would be all right by him, it would be only a just chastisement. But what dishonour the cowardice of His disciple would bring on the Master ! The court had the effect of a sepulchre, of a hell on him, it suffocated him.

"*He went in . . . to see the end*". It had ended sadly anyway as far as he was concerned. What support will his friendship be for Jesus ? He ought not to have come here. When the Master had warned him that he would end up by denying Him . . . . .

But no, it had not ended for him with his denials. The end was the Saviour's look. This look tormented him and reassured him at the same time. He wanted to dwell on this vision of forgiveness and hope. He fled outside, and there he wept bitterly !

Peter does not weep on account of his own misery, to weep for ourselves only makes our pride worse or increases our discouragement. The Apostle would have stayed inconsolable if he had only thought of his sin. But the melancholy that shakes his breast comes from the sorrow he caused Jesus and the harm that his example can cause to the other disciples when they learn that their leader failed.

For us, no less, repentance ought not to consist of cursing ourselves. We ought to suffer for having responded so poorly to the love that Jesus Christ bears us. We ought to deplore the bad example that we give to our brethren and the harm we do the Church. It is still not enough to pray with the sentiment of true contrition, one must go past the facile stage of emotion.

Jesu, labantes respice. Christ's look is a divine look, a " creative " look that can make a new soul out of us. But we must assist it and for that, we need not weep only, but following Peter's example, must *rise out* of the false and illogical situations which would inevitably give rise to a relapse. We must finish with imprudences, break with dangerous habits, give up a harmful friendship perhaps, leave the place where we would be inevitably conquered. These sacrifices are as costly as they are indispensable, also, to enable us to achieve them, let us look towards the Lord Who is looking at us. We sin because we forget His presence.

One of the privileges of the Christian (I am speaking of the man who is conscious of his baptism) is that he cannot live tranquilly while in sin. The discrepancy between his conduct and his faith provokes in him a sad disequilibrium, which he flatters himself vainly he can escape by opting for sin. Jesus Christ loves us too much to tolerate our ruin, we will never be at peace with sin, He will always claim us because we belong to Him.

Not only can we not look for a cheating forgetfulness in sin, but the Christian (and I am still speaking of the man who has truly loved our Lord) does not even know sin in the same way others do. Very often, when we receive confidences of the faults of our poor brothers who love our Lord, we are struck by the awkwardness with which they sin. " *Et tu Galilaeus es !* " Their accent betrays them, their Christian character comes through in their attitudes, their words or their silences. A Christian is not made to sin, he will fall, like Peter, unexpectedly, through weakness, but this is also why he can raise himself up again.

The only thing is that we end up by swinging from one extreme to another. After an excessive confidence in ourselves that makes us neglect the elementary precautions of prudence, once experience has shown us our weakness, we pass brusquely to an exaggerated diffidence that makes us doubt the possibility of our ever rising again. Before we believed too strongly, " there is nothing to fear ! " Then after our defeat, our will is overthrown, " I will never be able ! " At first we believed ourselves incapable of ever falling down, the next thing was we were saying that we were powerless to recover the lost ground and to advance. These successive states of presumption and discouragement are not contradictory, although they seem to be. They both arise out of the same love of self. Sure of ourselves or uncertain of ourselves, whichever it is, it is only ourselves we are thinking of.

Peter fell into the first trap, but he was able to avoid the second because in the meantime the Lord looked at him. Immediately he understood that distrustfulness is not the true corrective for presumption, but that confidence is what is always needed, except that it must be placed in God and not in oneself.

" *And Peter went out and wept bitterly* . . " Where did he go ? It never occurred to him to rejoin the other Apostles. Could he have faced Mary so soon after denying all knowledge of her Son ? He needed to be alone, and he went blindly forward, starting with sorrow every time the silence of the day, that was breaking, was shattered by the crowing of a cock. I should like to think that he went back towards Gethsemani, now empty, and sobbing threw himself down, there, where he had not been able to watch one hour, on the rock that was still stained with the blood of the Agony.

Now the sun is up, the sun of Good Friday, the sun of God's forgiveness for men. Among the olive trees, Peter is still weeping.

But far away, near a fig-tree, to which a belt is already tied, other sobs are racking the breast of another Apostle. Judas too is weeping because of his crime, and there is nothing sham about his desolation. Bolder even than Simon Peter, he was not afraid to face Jesus' enemies. He confessed his guilt and his Master's innocence publicly. And when the Elders and the priests jeered at him, he threw the pieces of silver, that were burning his fingers, on to the floor of the Temple. And he too went out, and he wept bitterly also. "*I have sinned in betraying the blood of an innocent man!*"

Why did God's forgiveness (as far as we know) not descend on Judas? What was lacking in his repentance? Repentance itself! That is just what he lacked. His feeling was only shame. Poor Judas lacked a glimmer of hope, an ounce of love; what he needed was to go and beg for Jesus' look.

Who knows, Christians, whether we won't give way to-morrow? May God keep us from making our sin irremissible by doubting His love! But no, we will not fall, if we keep a sincere regret for yesterday's faults in our hearts, if we stay close to Peter and keep watching **Jesus.** *Jesu, labantes respice* . . . .

CHAPTER XXII

TO THINK WITH THE CHURCH

The Lord has indeed risen and has appeared to Simon.
(Luke XXIV, 34).

UNTIL the Resurrection, Simon was one of us. Throughout the whole long education that the Master made him undergo, we could recognise qualities analagous to our own in his generosity, his lack of understanding and his relapses into self-love. Such are the qualities that attract us to the Saviour's person and the beauty of His doctrine, such also are those qualities that make us hesitate before the rigours of His law. Even afterwards when Jesus had promised him the fundamental place he would hold in His Church, we still find our own weakness in him. He resembled ourselves, all the time. He resembles us to such an extent that we see him sinning like ourselves.

But from Easter Sunday on, Peter moves on to a superior plane. We will have, of course, to wait for the miracle of Pentecost to bring about the total transformation that the Holy Ghost had to work in him. Already however, he is " the head ", he exercises the prerogatives of that position, he assumes its responsibilities.

The tears he shed after his fall purified his charity of any remains of egoism that might get mixed up in it still. No longer would his faith translate itself into the manifestations of enthusiasm that had so often led him astray. If Jesus prayed for His Apostle's faith, it was not only that it might not waver in times of trial, but that it might become more reflective, more profound, incapable of erring any more.   Peter's faith was now the faith of the Church.

When the two disciples, on Easter Sunday evening, who had just returned suddenly from Emmaus, knocked on the door of the house where the reunited Apostles were to be found, they wanted to let them know how Jesus had joined them on the way and how they had recognised Him at the breaking of bread. But before they could open their mouths, the others told them that they knew the marvellous news already. " *The Lord has indeed risen and has appeared to Simon* ".

That morning, the holy women's stories instead of persuading the Apostles, had made them more perplexed. But this evening, they knew. " *The Lord appeared to Simon* ". Isn't it funny, that although they have no difficulty in giving credence to Peter's word, when they in their turn are confronted with the evidence their confidence seems to waver? Some moments later, in fact, the risen Saviour shows Himself to all those who are in the room, then, they are gripped by terror, they are frightened of being cheated, they think that their imagination is making fun of them. Jesus lets them touch His hands and His feet, but they are so moved that they cannot believe it is true. In order to convince them completely, the Master must eat in their presence . . . . . . They did not believe their eyes, it was easier for them to believe the testimony of Peter. *Apparuit Simoni*, there is the basis of their faith.

The Saviour has still lots of other proofs of His Resurrection for them. He will collect them together for calmer conversations than in their dear Galilee, He will make them return to Jerusalem. At every fresh meeting during those forty days, He will talk to them of the Kingdom of God. These repeated favours will strengthen their faith, but that faith's point of departure was the apparition to Simon !

St. Paul has preserved a fragment of the creed that the Apostles made the first converts learn and that he himself learned. " Christ, as the Scriptures had foretold, died for our sins, he was buried, and then rose again on the third day " .... The formula then catalogues the principal apparitions, particularly the one that took place before more than five hundred of the brethren, most of whom were still living twenty years later, but the one that the *Credo* of the first Christians puts at the head of the list is the apparition to Simon, " and then, as the Scriptures had foretold, (He) rose again on the third day. *That he was seen by Cephas,* then by the eleven Apostles " [1].

Visus est Cephae. If we were writing a book of apologetics, we would insist on the force that this simple affirmation gives to the historical truth of the fact of the Resurrection, for it withdraws all scientific basis from the fairy-tales invented by the rationalists to try and explain how the Apostles, whom Jesus' death had plunged into utter dejection of spirit, could gradually come to believe that their Master must live for ever. The unconscious workings of collective mythomania would require at least several days if not a few weeks. But, forty-eight hours after the Saviour had been placed in the tomb, the Apostles pass suddenly from the most complete confusion to certainty in His Resurrection. One event changed the course of their thoughts instantaneously : "*He was seen by Cephas !*" Peter's testimony determined the faith of the young Church.

It is no less interesting to follow the developments within the soul of the Apostle himself. On the morning of the third day, the eleven with some disciples were gathered together, probably to agree upon their line of conduct now that the Gospel had apparently been defeated, when the women, who had gone out to the

---

[1] I Cor., XV, 1–7.

tomb early that morning to see about embalming the
corpse, burst in on them. The Sepulchre had been
empty and angels, who looked like men clothed in a
dazzling light, had given them a message " *Go and tell
Peter and the rest of His disciples* . . . . " (So Peter was
actually singled out.)

When they repeated the words of the heavenly
messengers, Jesus' friends, instead of jumping with joy,
pitied the women's simplicity and refused to give
credence to what they described as " nonsense ".

But two Apostles, however, did not share in the general
incredulity. Peter got up immediately and ran to the
tomb. John accompanied him. Younger and more
active, the latter passed his companion and was the
first at the tomb, but he did not go in. It was Simon
Peter who went into the mortuary chamber. John's
recollections are precise and thanks to him we can
reconstruct the scene. The two Apostles noticed that
the Master's body had not been carried off somewhere,
for in that case He would have been taken just as He
had been placed there, wrapped in linen-cloths. Now,
Peter ascertained that the winding sheet had been
unrolled and thrown in a corner, the veil that had
covered His head was, on the contrary, lying in a different
spot. John came in to inspect in his turn, and he tells
us that from then on he was fully convinced : "*And he
saw and learned to believe*". He does not let us know
Peter's impressions, but they were not as definite.
According to the third Gospel, Peter came out, "*full
of surmise over what had befallen*".

This is certainly the first time that we have seen Simon
Peter waiting before expressing his opinion. He is now
the head who cannot make statements lightly. He
suspends his judgment, or at any rate, he does not make
it known. Perhaps it is because of his silence that John
preferred to be silent also. In fact, when they were

back among the disciples they kept a prudent reserve, which is why Cleophas and his friend decided it was pointless to prolong their stay in Jerusalem and so set out for Emmaus. Later they would tell the unknown traveller who was to join them on the road, " . . *Some of those who were with us went to the tomb, and found that all was as the women had said, but of him they saw nothing* ". But when they returned that night, the other disciples knew as much about it as they did, for in the interval the Lord had appeared to Simon.

Apparuit Simoni ! We must be content with those two words ! The other apparitions reported in the New Testament are accompanied by some details, we know nothing about this one. Peter is no longer the man who boasted that he was steadier than the others. How humble he has become after his fault ! He keeps the secret of that first meeting to himself. We can easily guess what he could have said to the Master, from his tear-stained eyes. What Jesus told him was, doubtless, intended for no other ears but his. Peter is no longer one of ourselves, he is now the Head, charged with strengthening his brethren in the faith. Peter *knows* that Jesus is risen, he *says* so and his brethren *believe*.

Not all however. On the evening of that very day " Thomas was not with them when Jesus came . . . "

*   *   *   *

There is no justification for regarding this absence of Thomas' as a fault ; it was, rather, a great misfortune for him. It was no use for the others to repeat that they had seen the Lord, that they had touched His scars and His wounds, Thomas stubbornly refused to believe. Cephas' testimony left him still incredulous.

It is, doubtless, so that we may learn to raise ourselves up again quickly from our weaknesses, Brethren, that God permitted these temporary errors of two Apostles in those decisive days for Christianity. The first, unfaithful to Jesus Christ, the second, disbelieving the Church, both of them were converted by the Saviour's merciful condescendence, and both of them made reparation for their passing weakness, by a sublime act of charity, " *Thou knowest all things ; thou canst tell that I love thee* ", said Simon and Thomas declared, " *My Lord and my God !* "

Peter and Thomas have, besides, more than one trait in common, they are both generous, ardent, and impulsive.

When, for fear of the Jews who had threatened to stone Him, the disciples were dissuading the Master from going to Bethany, where Lazarus was so sick, Thomas, like Peter in the Cenacle later on, was ready to brave the danger. " *Let us go too* ", he said to the others, " *and be killed along with him !* " [1]

When the Lord announces His imminent departure to them, Thomas' impulsive character shows itself once more. As Peter wanted to follow Jesus, Thomas wants to know the way to rejoin Him. It was his question which earned for us the ravishing reply from the Lord, " I am the way ; I am truth and life " [2]. Like Peter, he was not afraid to make himself stand out, " Though all should desert you, I will not ", the former had said, the latter cried, " Until I have put my finger into the mark of the nails, you will never make me believe " [3].

Thomas' obstinacy must certainly have caused Peter pain, reviving in him the sad memory of the stubborness he had shown and for which he had paid so dearly ! Torn between his mission to strengthen his brethren in the faith and the humility he felt at meeting his own faults in those of his companion, how he must have

---

[1] John, XI, 6–16.
[2] John, XIV, 5.
[3] John, XX, 25.

prayed for the unbeliever! Must it not have been in response to Peter's prayer that the Lord consented, after a week's delay, to show His wounds to the doubting Apostle?

Jesus does not, however, present Himself to him separately. Thomas had been the victim of doubt because " he was not with them ", but eight days later " *Thomas was with them* ", with Peter, with the Church. Then Jesus reappeared and the Apostle who had demanded that he put his hand in the wound in His side blushed at his own pretentious pride. He did not stretch out his hands to touch the risen Master, he joined them to adore his Lord and his God!

Thomas lost eight days, eight days of peace, eight days of joy! How happy he was now! But Jesus remarked to him, would he not have been happier still, if he had believed, without having seen? If, like the others, he had believed Peter's word. *Apparuit Simoni!*

*   *   *   *

We have had occasion to observe before that, from the very beginnings of the Church, Peter exercised an uncontested authority. What took place in the dawn of the pascal feasts, even before the total outpouring of the Holy Ghost on the Apostles, shows us that the head of the Church already enjoyed the special assistance that keeps the faith from all error.

With the development of the Church, the privilege of the doctrinal infallibility of the Vicar of Jesus Christ will receive its precise definition. We only note that in those first days when Peter took the Master's place (He was always present though invisible) among his brethren, he did not make any mistakes.

One might have expected an abrupt reaction from

Peter on discovering the empty tomb. The impulsive
Apostle was not always master of himself. *Abiit secum
mirans* . . . . . He is astonished, he wonders, he reflects,
he waits. If we were told that this unusual moderation
of the Apostle's was the result of the sorrow that racked
him, we would recognise in it more the action of God
Who, as St. Paul writes, sees to it that " everything
helps to secure the good of those who love God " [1],
everything, even their faults.

Aroused by the reports of the holy women, Peter
does not accord them a blind belief, but he does not
take the exception that the others, apart from John,
take to them. He is in a hurry to find out and he runs
to the sepulchre. There, he observes everything
scrupulously, but he does not jump to conclusions.
Abiit secum mirans. He did everything humanly possible
for finding out the truth. It was up to Another now
to put him onto the final stage of his researches. It
was up to the Lord to enlighten him as He had promised.
And the Lord appeared to him.

God possesses a thousand ways of maintaining the
head of His Church in the truth, and miraculous interventions will not always be the means chosen by
Providence. However Peter's successor, whoever he
is, will always walk in the ways of truth.

History repeats itself indefinitely, for the events,
among which the destiny of men is played out, are subject
to the eternal laws of the Creator. Before St. Peter,
St. John was certain that Jesus had risen : " *Then the
other disciple* . . . . *also went in, and saw this and learned to
believe* ". · But John respected Peter's reflections. Thomas
did not accept Simon's testimony, nor that of his brethren,
he quibbled, he argued, he grew stubborn. For his
own personal conviction, he claimed to be allowed to
judge by himself. His hesitations teach us a valuable

---

[1] Rom., VIII, 28.

lesson, but for him they only lost time, sooner or later he would have to come round to Peter's judgment if he was to remain a disciple and apostle of Christ. It will always be the same in the Church. Some go forward, some lag behind. Peter walks in time with the Holy Ghost. Peter's successor, the Man in White, speaks the necessary words at the proper moment. He knows how to wait for that hour without impatience, but when Peter spoke, woe to the man who did not want to hear him. Subterfuges or evasions, tenacious interpretations, appeals to a better informed pope, we know, alas, where these delaying tactics lead : outside the Church. One only "thinks with the Church", by listening filially to the Head whom God has given it. Not content with adhering without discussion to the decisions of her infallible master, but even when the successor of St. Peter merely gives counsel and advice, let us accept it also, Brethren, with confidence and without reserve. To put it aside, would certainly be to put ourselves astray. If we followed it, we would always be on the path of truth.

CHAPTER XXIII

THE ESSENTIAL CONDITION OF THE APOSTOLATE

Simon, son of John, dost thou care for me more than these others ?

(John XXI, 15).

How often, Brethren, in the short time that the graces, which follow the reception of the Sacrament of Penance, are working in us, has each of us not found comfort in meditating on the words that Jesus and Peter exchanged after the apparition on the shores of Lake Tiberias ! Are we not then the pardoned sinner who does not dare pronounce phrases of fidelity any more, after having been so often unfaithful ? And yet we can bear witness to the sincerity of our affection for the Master who knows our innermost secrets. " *Lord, thou knowest all things, thou canst tell that I love thee* ".

Remember however, that though it is permissible for us to transpose it into our personal life, the dialogue that St. John reports deals with a situation that is strictly confined to Simon Peter only.

Jesus' three questions : " Simon, son of John, dost thou care for me?" are not meant to assure him that his fault is forgiven. Jesus gave this certainty to him on Easter Sunday, in a special apparition. One cannot say, either, that by offering Peter a chance to declare publicly the great affection he holds for Him, Jesus only wanted to re-establish the guilty Apostle in the eyes of his companions in the Apostolate. Without doubt, the Saviour's triple interrogation could not fail to remind him of his triple denial, and although that word was not mentioned, and no direct allusion had been made to his failing, Peter himself connects the three oaths that Jesus asks of him, with the three times he had denied all knowledge of Him in the house of Caiphas. And he cannot disguise his sorrow, when for the third time, Jesus questions him, " Simon, son of John, dost thou love me ? " " *Contristatus est Petrus !* "

However even if Our Lord did want to allow Peter to make reparation for his sin, this was not the sole nor the principal intention He had in posing the same question to him three times in succession. The aim of this repetition was to underline the gravity of the promises with which the Saviour replied to those of the converted Apostle. If Jesus asked him three times " Dost thou love me ? " it was so as to repeat to him three times, " Be the shepherd of my flock ! " and so as to make more solemn the investiture of Peter in the redoubtable charge that He gave him of guiding the Church in His name. For it was then that Peter was really " consecrated " head of the Church. The Son of God was going to hand over His divine powers to a man. Should not this unforgetable hour in the history of the salvation of humanity be attended by a ceremonial that would bring out its grandeur ?

But it was necessary too that this " consecration " of the head of the Church should be presented to Peter and the other Apostles as the coronation of the Saviour's minister among them. This explains the choice of the circumstances in which Jesus wished it to take place.

Notice the setting. It is the shores of Lake Genesareth where the youth of the four first Apostles had been passed, it was there that they had practised their trade until the day that Jesus had entered into their lives. It was on this Lake that the miraculous draught of fishes had happened, following which the disciples left their boats and nets to follow Him who wanted to make them fishers of men.

It was at this same place that the risen Saviour came to wait for them. The necessity of living had forced them to fall back on their old trade, they had gone out fishing. And this night, like the other, they had caught nothing and were coming back in the early morning, and this time again it was at a word from Jesus that, casting their nets once more, they brought it out loaded with one hundred and fifty-three great fish.

John, the intuitive one, had quickly identified the voice that had said to them " Cast to the right of the boat ! " and Peter, the impulsive one, hurled himself into the water so as to be the first at His Master's side. Then the disciples surrounded Him. They shared a bit of bread and grilled fish with Him. This was the end of fishing on the lake. In future, they would be fishers of men. As the Father had sent the Son, so the Son was sending them. Their mission was immense, to go throughout the whole world, preaching the Gospel to all creatures. Their task will never end. Jesus is with them all days even to the end of the world.

But a visible head must take His place. At Cesarea, Jesus had designated Peter for this office, the moment has arrived to enthrone him in it in reality. Jesus liked to compare Himself to a shepherd, who knows all his sheep, one by one, and whose voice they all know—a shepherd who shows the way by walking in front of his flock—who feeds his flock, giving them life, a super-abundant life and who, from time to time, seems to neglect the faithful flock, to leave them without food and without water, in order to run in search of a lost sheep . . . . Now Jesus has finished His earthly tasks, He hands His shepherd's crook to Peter, He confides His sheep and His lambs to him, His whole flock, His Church.

But before establishing him finally at the head of all the disciples, the Saviour recalls to him three times the indispensable quality He expects of him if he is to represent Him on earth, to speak in His name, to attract men and to lead them to God. "*Simon, son of John, dost thou care for me more than these others ?*"

If Jesus chose Peter to become the head of His Church it is because Peter loved Him and was capable of loving Him more than the others. Jesus did not make a similar commendation of anyone else. But the love He was talking of, was not of the purely sentimental kind. Jesus said so, many times. He who loves accomplishes the will of the Father, he observes the commandments. Will Peter obey Him from now on more than anyone else ? Will he do the will of God more than anyone ? The Church is founded on Peter's obedience to Jesus Christ. On this condition the very life of the Church depends. All the disciples are bound to obey Peter, but Peter will obey Jesus not just as much, but more than the others. The fundamental law of the Church is obedience, the faithful obey the Pope and the Pope obeys Christ " more than the others ".

This is why our Lord asks Peter for an oath of absolute fidelity, a vow of total allegiance. So grave is the pledge that Peter is going to undertake before taking over the leadership of the Church, that Jesus formulates it to him three times in succession. And three times in succession, Peter is consecrated head of the Church, as later his successors will wear the Triple Crown.

* * * *

What were Simon Peter's feelings at this time ? Perhaps we can disentangle them from the very simple terms of his replies.

At the first question, the Apostle still does not know

for what reason Jesus is asking him " *Dost thou care for me more than these others ?* " Besides, the question is a peculiar one anyway. It would have been understood clearly if the Lord had meant to say " Dost thou care for me more than thou carest for these others ? " but such a question would have been indeed frivolous and would not have been worth posing. Not alone for Peter, but for all the Apostles, Jesus was, without comparison, the person they loved best in the world. The question is therefore the one we did not expect. Jesus is really asking Peter if he loves Him more than the other disciples love Him. We would not hesitate, Brethren, to admit that we love the woman who is our mother in a unique degree and manner. But would you not be embarrassed if someone pressed you to declare that you loved your mother more than your brothers did ? One cannot say that. First of all, one does not know, and secondly if it were true, could you say it in front of your brothers ? And yet Jesus submits Simon Peter to a test like this. In public, before six other Apostles, among whom is St. John, who calls himself so simply in his Gospel " the disciple whom Jesus loved ", the Master asks Peter whether he is more devoted, more attached to Him than the others.

Do not let us think, however, that our Lord wanted to pose His Apostle an embarrassing question. The question is not, it could not be, " Do you think the others love me less than you do ? " He asks him, " Are you decided not to take as a scale for your affection, the generosity of the most generous of your brethren, but *to will* to love me more than those who love me the most, that is to say, to go beyond all measure ? . . . . You received more than the others, you are invested with higher functions than theirs, can I expect from you a higher devotion than theirs ? . . . . Perhaps you also understand that you must sacrifice yourself in my service more than these others, because you have to make reparation for a fault that these others did not commit ? "

Peter is not long in replying ! *More than the others ?* These words awake in him, the memory of a sorrow that will never leave him more. He was not more valiant than the others during the Lord's Passion, he was more imprudent. Yes, his rashness made him fall into a fault that the others did not commit . . . . Peter does not want to compare himself to his brethren any more although he is ready to suffer more than they. We should admire the *humility* of his reply. He begs the Saviour Himself to judge his dispositions. " *Yes, Lord, thou knowest well that I love thee !* "

The other Apostle listened to Simon's humble reply which carefully avoided placing himself above them. They also heard the words with which Jesus confirmed in Peter the powers He had promised to him earlier on. " *Feed my lambs !* " All understand the Saviour's intentions now. Peter, in particular, grasped the sense of this " more than these others " which had intrigued them. The head—Jesus had often taught it to him— ought to serve more than the others, more perfectly, more completely, more humbly. The more numerous the souls that Jesus confides to us, the more we ought to love Him.

Is it not surprising also that Jesus repeats His question now that all have discovered its meaning ? But Jesus will spare Peter's humility by making no further allusion to the others, for the second time He only asks " *Simon, son of John, dost thou care for me ?* "

It is possible that the Lord would like to invite him to renew his old resolutions but Peter never retracted them in the depths of his heart, even when his lips were lying in an hour of madness. Is it not rather towards the future that the Lord is directing His Apostle's thoughts, towards the mission with which He is charging him ? Certainly, Peter could protest aloud of his henceforth indefectible fidelity ; he will love the Saviour with more force than if he had no fault to expiate. Besides, the circumstances are no longer the same. When Peter failed Him, the tragic events of the Passion had thrown a disquieting veil over the divinity of the Saviour. But in triumphing over death, the risen Jesus gives them a stunning proof of His divinity, and the latter threw light at last on the workings of the Redemption, which had been obscure for His disciples, so difficult that they did not want to believe it, when Jesus explained its mysterious laws to them. Henceforth, their faith will not be able to waver. Peter would therefore be able to affirm that he is ready to undertake the new work that Jesus is assigning to him, but he will never again rely on himself. Jesus alone knows whether he will be able to fulfil it well, and Jesus will help him to do so. " *Lord, thou knowest well that I love thee !* " And the Master blesses His Apostle's *trust.* " *Tend my shearlings !* "

Why does Jesus prolong the test again ? Peter asks himself this sadly when he is questioned for the third time. The other Apostles do not recognise any more the old bubbling ardour of the companion who, in the old days, would have flown into a passion at the Saviour's insistence. Could Jesus doubt Peter ? This supposition, which would have made the Apostle jump only a few days before, not only does not provoke any revolt in him, but what is more admirable, does not succeed in discouraging him. In such a situation, what would we not have done ? Would we not have retired, saying to the Master, " You can choose someone worthier than me ? " Peter does not return the keys to the Master, Who seems uncertain of his affection, and that is, without doubt, the greatest victory be could win over his self-love.

Deeply hurt, he does not show any impatience. To humility and trust, he adds this time an act of total

abandonment, "*Lord, thou knowest all things . . . . .!*
You know my good will, but also the faults of my
character that you took me up on many times, you know
my weakness, you know that I fled and that I disowned
you ; you know the difficulties of the task to which you
have called me. You know better than I whether I
can lead my brethren, You, who read in my heart,
Thou canst tell that I love thee ! "

And the Saviour, before Whom the future opens out
like an open book, proclaims for the last time God's
boldest plans, which are not afraid to hand over to a
man the eternal destinies of all humanity : "*Feed my
sheep !* "

* * * *

Brethren, having regard to the necessary adaptations,
we can in ending, draw the lesson, which in this scene
as grave as it is touching, is addressed to all Christians.

It is not the least mystery of our religion, that God
wants the love of His creatures, " *Dost thou love me ?* "
How can He have this desire, this need for our affection ?
But it is also the privilege of our religion, and what puts
it above all others, that it makes us capable of loving
God, because Jesus Christ, God made man, can be the
object of our affection.

How this love for Jesus has raised and sanctified
humanity ! For love of Jesus, the child learns to master
his instincts, the invalid to put up with his suffering,
the martyr has the strength to renounce life and, which
is no less astounding, the sinner can rise out of his sin.

" *Dost thou love me ?* " Our Lord does not pose this
question only to men who obey His commandments.
He lets those who neglect Him or betray Him hear
the same appeal. God does not consider it lowering
Himself to beg the sinner for his love. Also, when the

latter repents, let him not think himself, because of his faults, unworthy of the intimacy that Jesus Christ proposes to him. As the Abbé of Tourville wrote, " Our Lord is not the Master, who is concerned with the good pupils only [1]. He offers us this sweet means of making reparation for our faults : Loving. To love the Saviour whom we have denied. To love the prayer that we have given up. To love the truth wounded by our lies. To love our duty in loving him who orders us.

But it is very especially from apostolic souls that Jesus expects affection. *Amas me ? . . . . Pasce oves meas.* Who would be surprised at this ? Proselytism can only be born out of love. The ardour of our convictions compels us to spread them; can we admire anyone without wanting everyone to admire them with us ? An apostle who does not love, what a contradiction in terms ? An apostle who loves himself more than Christ, the man who is out for himself, is no more, in short, than an empty wine-skin. An apostle will only be able to persuade and win over others if the love of Jesus overflows in his life—and not only from his lips.

Observe however that the Christian who has sinned is not excluded from apostolic tasks. If he loves our Lord again, he too can make Christ's flock increase. Although he had sinned, Peter threw himself into the water to arrive at the Master's side more quickly, and he was the consecrated prince of the Apostles. Can we make better reparation for our faults than by devoting ourselves to souls in order to snatch them from error or from evil and to lead them to Jesus Christ ?

This gift of ourselves, Jesus wants it unceasingly and always more fully. Do not let us congratulate ourselves that we have already made it, do not let us judge ourselves falsely by comparing ourselves to those who do less than we ; we ought to love Him always and more

---

[1] *Piété confiante*, p. 301.

than others . . . . . It would be madness on our part to think that we could become sinless. Jesus does not expect it. Our negligences, our forgetfulness, our very relapses astonish Him less than they do us. It is not three times, but a hundred times and more that we oblige Him to renew His prayer, " *Dost thou love me ?* " And we are right to be sad, but let us not lose confidence. The attraction of sin is diminished in proportion to the love we bear our Lord. Let us repeat daily the words that kept Peter from falling again, " Lord, You know all things, my faults of yesterday, my weakness of to-day, my temptations of to-morrow, You know also how much I love you ! "

CHAPTER XXIV

THE BONDS THAT LIBERATE

*But when thou hast grown old, thou wilt stretch out
thy hands, and another shall gird thee, and carry
thee where thou goest, not of thy own will.*

(John XXI, 18.)

PETER is now the supreme pastor of the Church. His
faithful and tender affection for Jesus will make him
capable of fulfilling the duties of his charge. The
Apostle has abandoned himself completely to his Lord's
choice. But the Latter just points out for him the extent
of the abandonment that He expects from His representative on earth, " *Believe me when I tell thee this ; as a
young man thou wouldst gird thyself and walk where thou
hadst the will to go* ".

Jesus puts in opposition the two ages of life. On the
one hand, there is the young man who only acts as he
wishes, he goes wherever he wants, he is free in his
decisions, free also in his movements. He does not need
anyone to help him tuck up his garment and tighten
his belt. The old man, on the other hand, has neither
the same independence nor suppleness. Dependent on
those around him, he can no longer go where it seems
nice to him, he can no longer even gather together the
folds of his clothes, to set out walking or to begin work.
Someone else must tie his belt on him, and he stretches
out his arms, while they gird his loins. " *But when thou
has grown old, thou wilt stretch out thy hands and another
shall gird thee and carry thee where thou goest, not of thy own
will* ". And the Saviour adds, " *Follow me !* "

It is certainly the Head's business to take the initiative

and the responsibility for all decisions, but his commandments ought not to be arbitrary. He is not to order just what pleases him. He decides what he must decide, in conformity with truth and justice, keeping in mind the mission he has been given and the good of those over whom he exercises authority. More than anyone the Head of the Church must free himself from any point of view or influence that is subjective. He cannot lead the disciples as he likes, his first and foremost duty is to bring them into Christ's train. Less than any other leader, is the Head of the Church authorised to do what he wants. He is narrowly bound to Jesus Christ : "*Follow me*".

The years will not loosen the bonds that tie Peter to the Lord. Far from it, when he is old, he will give the final testimony of his obedience by dying the same death as his Master. The precision of this slightly obscure oracle of the Saviour's is noted in parenthesis by the Evangelist writing in the last years of the first century. "*So much he told him, prophesying the death by which he was to glorify God*". The second Christian generation knew how the first head of the Church had ended his Apostolate. Crucified as Jesus had been, he had stretched out his arms while they were attaching him to a cross.

At the time that the risen Saviour was speaking like this, the details of His prediction were naturally not so clear. However, all had a presentiment that Peter was destined to make the bloody sacrifice of his life. Peter, always the first, had understood this well for, his glance alighting on St. John just then, he asked the Master whether his friend would share in his lot. Jesus refuses to reply to this pointless question, " *What is it to thee ? Do thou follow me !* "

It is on these three words that Simon Peter's story ends in the Gospel. His novitiate is over. Soon the second part of his life will open out. Under his direction the Church, which continues Christ's life, will begin the conquest of the world. The whole programme of the head of the Church, like the whole secret of his interior life, is contained in these four words : " *Do thou follow me !* "

The words of farewell with which Jesus leaves him are exactly the words of his calling, heard on this same shore of Lake Genesareth—more personal however, and more pressing. It is no longer just " *Follow me* " but " *Do thou follow me !* "

What do the others matter to thee ? I am talking of thee, whom I have chosen, whom I have saved, whom I have taken and whom I keep. Do thou, Peter, follow Me. Me, whom thou lovest, Me whose true nature thou knowest, the Son of God become son of man, the Redeemer of all men whom I wish to make sons of God.

Thou with me ! Being alone no longer, thou shalt therefore fail no longer. When thou shalt speak, thou shalt say what I think and I wish. When thou shalt undergo trials, I shall keep thee in peace. Thou and I ! God is no longer invisible and far from men; I have come close to you, I have lived among you, and thanks to thee, all men will be able to live in Me.

For I am thy law, thy strength, thy reward and thou art the hope of God for men. Between thee and Me, the Church will stand and the salvation of all men will be made possible.

Do not let thyself be influenced by desires, by fears or by human interests. Human views will be ascribed to thee. Some will reproach thee for thy intolerance, others for thy opportunism. Let them talk. " *Do thou follow me !* " Follow Me only ! Because thou wilt follow Me, thy brethren will not go astray, thy conduct will be a model for theirs. Since thou hast prayed it of Me, I have promised thee that there, where I am going, thou shalt follow Me later. Later, in fact, when thou hast grown old, thou wilt stretch out thy hands like I, to die as I did, in order to follow Me and find Me again in the Church of heaven.

* * * *

What the Gospel lets us know of Simon Peter's story stops on the threshold of his career as leader. We have only gone over the principal stages of his formation, trying each time to draw some profit for ourselves from the lessons which he received from the Master. Peter should be accompanied through the rest of his apostolate, in order to admire how at a certain point his courageous amenableness to the Saviour's teachings makes him arrive at an effective sanctity. At least, leaving him prematurely, we will agree perhaps that his examples have made us more Christian and more Catholic, I mean more attached to Jesus Christ and more trustful in the Church. May this be our final resolution, in any case, since it is the one Jesus gave him in the form of a farewell (a farewell which was not a separation but the promise of a permanent intimacy), " *Do thou follow me !* "

To follow Jesus, to follow the Church, that, if you reflect on it, Brethren, is a decision to which Providence is leading us unceasingly. If we look back over our past years, we will recognise that the prediction announced to Simon when Jesus is taking leave of him, is being realised for all Christians all the time. Each of us has had experience of these unexpected interventions of " someone stronger than ourselves " which changed the course of our desires and thoughts abruptly and impressed on our life a new orientation that we had not foreseen.

In proportion as we advance in age, we go less and

less where we want, another takes us, another leads us, another binds us to duties which we would not have chosen ourselves and brings us, as it were in spite of ourselves, to a more christian life.

Cum esses junior. Is there anyone among you who has not, in his youth, dreamt of independence and freedom ? But the attempts made to realise it bring in the end only bitterness and sadness. " *Cum autem senueris . . .* " Victims of their own indiscipline, they have now stretched out their hands to let themselves be led by a Master who is better than themselves.

Our whole life as Catholics is only an interrupted series of divine calls, the continual repetition of " *Do thou follow me !* " You heard this call of Christ's when you hesitated to recognise, and above all to follow, the path of duty. Jesus repeated to your conscience, which was worrying about what choice to make, or worse still, was at grips with the calculations of interest or of pleasure, " *Do thou follow me !* " He faced you with the laws of the Church, whose clearcut formulae have preserved the divine wishes in all their purity.

Cum esses junior. But you were young, you looked at those who, having left Christ, boasted that they had shaken off constraints and scruples. Their apparent liberty made you envious. You too found yourself, like Peter, at the cross-roads, and Christ said to you " And you, are you going to leave me also ? " You did not throw yourself like the Apostle towards Him whose words give eternal life, you followed the disciples who went away . . . . But our Lord did not abandon you. He tormented you while you thought to enjoy your liberty, in your heart discouragement alternated with remorse, after growing ashamed of yourself, you lost hope in yourself, and to forget your troubles, you relapsed into your fault. But Christ did not accept the decadence to which you seemed to have consented. He will never accept that the branches cut off from the vine should wither and die.

Do thou follow me! He tormented you until you came and asked His forgiveness. A new ligature re-grafted you to the True Vine, you stretched out your hands. To load them with chains? No, but to grasp the rope that pulls the drowning man to the surface. In submitting yourself to the divine law, you won the true liberty, for the true liberty consists in being master of oneself. But to be master of oneself, you had to understand in the end that one must let oneself be bound and enclosed by Another, and go where one would not want to go.

Cum esses junior. Others have known a different struggle. Less embarrassed by the moral law than by Christian dogma, they were subjected during the years of adolescence, when one is so proud of thinking by onesefl, to the influence of systems of thought which deny the spirit of man. Catholic dogma seems to them something of the past that went against the teachings of history and contradicted the facts of science. They gave up Christian dogma to go and look for the truth on their own. In this long pilgrimage to all the sources of human knowledge they found nothing however that assuaged their thirst, going from one teaching to another like " children, storm-tossed . . . . driven before the wind of each new doctrine ", (the image is from St. Paul ;[1]) they only ended with doubt and dispairing agnosticism.

Cum esses junior. Or again, some, who were obedient to Jesus Christ's dogma and law, complained about the disciplines of the Church. When one is young, one finds that everything in the world is wrong, one is in a hurry to reform it, and you discovered, perhaps, that the Church was rather slow to act, when faced with

---

[1] Eph., IV, 14.

the hardness of human societies that were rebelling against the divine ferment of justice, that she seemed to be sharing in an evil, which at the same time she, theoretically, was condemning. You looked for other methods, You gave yourself to other leaders who promised you a more rapid success. The struggle into which they led you is not over, you did not win any victory in it— the triumph of force is never a victory.

Cum autem senueris. Later you understood that in order to conquer the world and put it in order, it was first necessary that we should have conquered ourselves, that we should have put ourselves in order. It is not a bolder Church that will save the earthly city (so many men to-day are beginning to discover her boldness), it is a holier church that will be able to push back sin, the first of all social disorders, a holier church, that is to say, composed of believers, who are more intransigent in their faith, but also more and more disinterested in their obedience to all the laws of the Church. One must always end by stretching out one's arms and being spread out on the cross.

*   *   *   *

Most of you, Brethren, have never revolted against the loving authority that Christ exercises over His Church. Conscientious Christians, exact in their duties to the state, courageous in labour, valiant under trial, you have arrived in the middle of life's way, and you look towards the future with the hope that your task will grow less arduous, and that you will know an epoch of lesser effort, if not a time of retirement, of rest, and recollection. But to you too, the Lord's words are applicable : " *Cum autem senueris* ".

The further one advances in life, the less one is free to shape it to one's will. Duties do not disappear, they only change and generally became more and more onerous. Another conducts our life and leads us where He wills.

The young mother holding her curly-headed child in her arms, can indulge in the nice silly dream that the young fellow will never grow up. "Why, dear baby, so sweet and simple, must you become a man, and be selfish, hard and violent like others". All this time, the child only dreams of growing up, he wants to be a man, he already gives himself airs when he is scarcely an adolescent. He wants to be free and that one word "freedom" can make his mother quake . . . . Then it is that Another comes and takes him by the hands, and leads him where he did not want to go.

He imposes the law of labour on him, which takes up his whole day and obliges him to create, to produce happiness for his brethren. He keeps him bound down to long preparations for careers that demand a more regular life. Another has bound him to work and has saved him, made holy by work. Christ put in his way, in your way, the man or the woman, whom He wished to join to your existence. He bound you both under the same yoke, no more freedom. ! But at the same time He freed you from the caprices of individualism. You tasted the charm of a home which soon sheltered a family. Children came to take away a little more of your individuality and your freedom, and with them your arms were certainly loaded with fetters, cares, hardship, suffering, worries . . . . . You said when they were young : later we will be our own masters. They grew up, they were your masters more than in the past. In middle age, the father and sometimes, the mother, are assailed by a need for relaxation, they feel like escaping the monotony of duty . . . . And you were forced to cling to the law, to continue your old life, to draw support from your religion, your children obliged you to do so. Another held you bound to duties, from which, without Him, you would perhaps have freed yourself.

Will it never come, the hour of retirement? If it does come it brings new duties in its train. After the children come the grandchildren. After your private affairs, care for public welfare and for good works. In order to fulfil these new duties, you have, no doubt, the resources of a wiser experience, but you no longer have the physical vigour of former days. Some are even deprived of the diversion that a new job would bring, they must begin their old tasks once more. The grandmother must start again with the education of little orphans. The father, after having worked all his life, has to take over the shaky business of a son or son-in-law. One must begin again, begin again until one can do no more. The Author is leading us all the time where we do not want to go.

If our activity suddenly stops, it is because the hour has come for the suffering which will be our personal reparation, which will, through our sacrifices, make fruitful the fields that the following generation is in the process of sowing in its turn. Besides, even before suffering immobilised us, we were laid low by other trials. Just notice it, what comes on us is never what we would have chosen. Dreams, poverty, mourning, deceptions, betrayals, there are so many unexpected trials, all of which seem so undeserved to us. They are the last steps on the way to sanctity, which God generally makes worse in the last stages of life (*Cum autem senueris*). But when we reply with the hard *Fiat* to the incomprehensible trial, our sufferings acquire a redeeming value. We raise ourselves above the earth with Christ, we begin to belong to heaven.

Cum autem senueris. Your spirits are now directed to the future. What does to-morrow hold for us? To-morrow, Brethren, we shall have grown old by one day, to-morrow Christ will bind us to another task, which will not be the one we foresaw, but which will save us and will make us greater.

A Christian ought not abandon himself to anguish and worry. Let us therefore resist, with the help of grace, the current panic that is looming up to-day and becoming so wide-spread. France is not done for. The Church is not done for. The Church must make France what she was in former days, a Christian nation. It is we, called by God at a providential hour, whom God is charging with this mission of love, to give France back the Christianity that made her, in the past, so great and so beautiful. There is no lack of prophets to tell us how, in their opinion, our dear country should be cured. The truth is that our country needs, first and foremost, more virtue. She needs God first of all. Since secularism chased God from our land, it is necessary that the " Catholic laity " should give Him back to her. Our country needs the virtue of all her Christians. We will regenerate her by infusing her with our Christian blood, and "infusing" may mean perhaps "spilling" . . . But afterwards ? " *What is it to thee ? Do thou follow me !* " Let us stretch out our hands and not let them fall down in a gesture of discouragement. Let us stretch out our hands to Christ so as to receive the task which He will give us day after day. Let us receive it with trust, let us perform it with courage. It is by following Him that we will win the others over, and that we will save ourselves, having shared in the salvation of the world.